Cheever, Harriet A

Little Mr. Van Vere of China

Cheever, Harriet A
Little Mr. Van Vere of China
ISBN/EAN: 9783743334007
Manufactured in Europe, USA, Canada, Australia, Japa
Cover: Foto ©ninafisch / pixelio.de

Manufactured and distributed by brebook publishing software (www.brebook.com)

Cheever, Harriet A

Little Mr. Van Vere of China

LIST OF ILLUSTRATIONS.

	PAGE
LITTLE MR. VAN VERE OF CHINA	*Frontispiece*
DONNY AND THE CAPTAIN	15
"'OH, PLEASE, MR. POLICE, DO LET TONY GO!' HE CRIED"	41
DONNY ON DECK	49
WILLING DONNY HELPED HER MORE AND MORE	83
"'THEY WON'T LET YOU RACE THE STREETS WILD ALL DAY NO LONGER'"	91
DONNY AS A STOWAWAY	109
"THERE STOOD A LITTLE BOY, WHITE AND SCARED"	115
JOCKO REFORMS	135
MR. RICHARD'S GARDEN	167
A TEMPLE OR JOSS-HOUSE	174
THE MANDARIN	191
"'YOU WERE THE FIRST MAN TO BE GOOD TO ME'"	205
"'HOW DO YOU DO, TONY?' SAID DONNY"	219
LITTLE MR. VAN VERE AT HOME AGAIN	231

LITTLE MR. VAN VERE OF CHINA.

CHAPTER I.

THE BRAND-NEW ONE.

Down the street raced Donny, his little ragged jacket fluttering in the wind. There had been almost no breakfast for him at Sunrise Court that morning, but small difference that made to the boy as long as the wharves with their beloved surroundings were open to his childish enjoyment.

It was later than Donny usually made his appearance, but granny Hilborn had wanted a number of errands done, and, as the child never thought of refusing to do anything granny asked of him, the October sun was high in the heavens as he flew along. All at once he stopped and looked eagerly as a little hawk at some object, fixing his gaze at a slight distance.

"Oh, my eye, that's a bran-new one!" he exclaimed,

softly, to himself. "She's a big three-masted one, too, I do b'lieve. Wonder where she's come from? Wonder wot's her name? Wonder wot does she bring?"

At this point of his wondering, Donny felt a sharp pull at one of his little tattered sleeves, and off came a large piece. Before he had time to say a word, there was a twitch at the back, and another fragment of the poor little jacket was gone.

"You stop now, Tony Winkers!" he cried, with more distress than anger in his voice. "You jus' stop spoilin' my jacket; it's all I got, and you jus' let me 'lone."

But a sly jerk here and there sent other bits of rag flying in the breeze. Donny began to cry.

"Oh, cry! cry real hard!" said the teasing big boy; "scream good now! louder, sonny, boo hoo! hoo! hoo! Why don't you try to make folks hear? then p'r'aps somebody'll come and rescue you."

But somebody was coming, and as a rude, cruel boy is almost always a coward, Mr. Tony Winkers all at once took to his heels, and ran around a near corner. Donny tried to stop crying. It wasn't nice to have people see his face all puckered up into a queer little shape, and tears rolling over his cheeks.

"Guess my jacket looks queer 'nough without my

face looking any queerer," thought the **forlorn** child. "'Fraid I sha'n't have 'nough left to **get into** pretty soon; then wot could I do 'bout the wharf?"

It was all hard enough for poor Donny without Tony Winkers's mean sport. The mornings are cold in October, and the bit of fire in granny Hilborn's little stove was scarcely hot enough to cook **the oatmeal**, of which there often was but very little, **very little indeed**. Then to have a boy's only jacket torn and pulled about until it was almost off his body was **too shameful**, and the tears would come into Donny's eyes as he hurried towards the wharf. Suddenly he came to a full stop again. "My! who *is* this? I sh'd think 'twas a Santa Claus, only 'tisn't his time. But my! isn't he the funny little man, though?"

It wasn't a little man at all that Donny saw coming, only he was so large round it made him look shorter than he was. But pitching and rolling along came the jolly figure, and as the twinkling **eyes**, bushy whiskers, and pleasant face came close to Donny, he noticed that the pockets of the large coat the man wore bulged out in queer nubbly bunches, as if **stuffed** with all kinds of good things for the stockings of rich little boys.

"Hey away there, little mate!" called a merry voice,

as the big figure came up to the thin, forsaken-looking child. "Quite weatherish this morning, isn't it, sir?"

Donny smiled, and two deep dimples showed in his cheeks. "Let's see," the merry voice went on, "are you the little chap — oh, now perhaps I'm mistaken! But is this the boy — bless me, I believe it is! — well, come now, am I right or wrong? Do you happen to be the little man I've heard of that likes oranges?"

Donny was going through a series of short little giggles as the bright eyes peered into his. Then he said, with a quiet little grin, "Yes, I likes oranges."

"Well, now, that's a mercy, because I started out thinking I might meet some little fellow that liked such things, and you see it's pretty hard to take myself around, and a parcel of oranges besides. Now suppose I should want to give a boy of about your size a couple of handfuls of oranges, what in the world could you do with them?"

The little street boy was not cornered for a moment. Off came his shabby little cap. The wind blew his soft light hair about his face, but that didn't trouble him for a moment. Into the cap, out from the bulging pockets, went six great oranges as yellow as gold.

"Any room for nuts?" asked the big man.

"Plenty," grinned Donny, and pattering like rain fell the nuts until the small cap would hold no more.

"Now if I only don't meet Tony Winkers again," said the boy, the smile dying out of his face as he looked anxiously around, "won't me and granny have a great time!"

"And who is Tony Winkers? Bless me, what a name! He ought to be an amazing boy for goodness carrying around such a name as that."

Donny's lip curled. "He tore the pieces out my jacket, and laughed when they went flying 'way. And he's big and strong; if I met him he'd grab all my nice things, and run off with them."

"Where's your home, little boy? Is it very far from here?"

"It's right in Sunrise Court, out o' the next street there."

"Very well, steer straight along. If Mr. Winkers appears, we'll speak a little piece."

Donny laughed and chuckled, and, hugging up his loaded cap, started for the court. At the entrance he looked back. The kind, jolly man waved his hand. Donny managed to wave his, and ran for granny's room.

CHAPTER II.

THE "OVERSEER."

"Oh, now, Donny, you ain't ever been fightin', I hope," cried granny Hilborn, at sight of the panting boy. "Do look at your jacket. It ain't fit to be seen. Now you'll have to stay indoors till I get time to mend you up a bit."

But the jacket just for a moment was not the first thing in Donny's mind. "Oh, look, granny, look!" he cried. "See what a big, nice man give me. He looked 'xactly like a Santa Claus, and he was all full o' laughin' with his eyes, and his pockets sticked way out all full o' goodies, and he watched so Tony Winkers wouldn't dare come and tear me all up again. Ain't those jolly oranges, granny?"

"Yes, the oranges is fine, but wot ever got your jacket? It's only half there."

"I met naughty Tony Winkers, and he kep' hitching pieces out my sleeves and back, and the more I cried the more he kep' a-teasin' at me."

"Ain't I tole you more'n a hundred times to keep out'n Tony Winkers's way?" snapped granny. "Now you mus' bide in the house till I finds some pieces. Ole Mis' Mellin said t'other day you looked like a rag-bag a-ready, and there sha'n't no chile o' mine go into the street half tore to bits."

How could Donny, with his pretty little dimpled face, fair hair, and blue eyes, be any relation to granny Hilborn? But then, no one knew much about any of the children in Sunrise Court, and granny was not really cross or unkind to Donny. She was too miserably poor to more than half feed the boy, and Donny had ways of picking up quite as much food as granny could get, so after all they helped each other. But the misery of having to stay indoors while granny found pieces to mend the torn jacket! Why, it might take her a week! Meantime there was the wonderful man who had turned up, and then, quite as important in the child's eyes, there was the smart, strange vessel at Holland Wharf.

"Oh, granny! granny!" he cried, "there's 'nother vessel come in yes'day, a bran-new one, and p'r'aps she's got lots o' good things on board I might get some of. I must run down and find out 'bout her, then I'll come right back if you say to. Sailors ain't goin' to notice 〰️a feller's got on; please be lettin' me go."

But granny was set. Mrs. Mellin wasn't going to call the boy she took care of a rag-bag, and with good reason. And Donny did look more like a bundle of rags than anything else with a garment on that had little dark flags waving all over it.

Yet the misery of it! Donny set his sharp little wits to work wondering how he could manage, for go to the wharf he must; but it never once entered his head to run away, — he somehow was not that kind of a child. The rest of the morning was a time of great sorrow for him. He tried to coax granny to take coarse thread, and bring together the parts of his jacket that remained; she said no, there wouldn't be room for him to half squeeze into it, if she mended that way. "Be whist now, and play horse or something," she said, "till I find pieces o' cloth; p'r'aps I might pick up a bit somewheres before long."

It seemed a hopeless case. Granny and Donny had a dinner of oranges, not an unusual thing, only they never were used to that kind of fruit. But the wharf was a great place for finding oranges, bananas, and various kinds of fruit that were tossed aside as unfit for the markets.

It seemed to the longing boy as though the afternoon would never wear away.

"Won't I have to go for bread by and by, granny?" he asked.

"No, I'll be gettin' Tom Smart to buy me a stale loaf when he goes for his own," was the discouraging reply.

It is a pity, but children often have to get along as best they can with disappointments, and Donny did not soon forget the long, hard day he passed without knowing what was going on at his place of business, as the wharf was to his mind. But granny dozed, swept a little, and appeared to do almost everything else except find pieces with which to mend him up. He tried hard to be patient, and, when night came, he laid on his pallet of straw thinking and planning, and planning and thinking, until something came to him that looked like a strong chance of helping himself out.

So the bright bird of Hope began singing in his heart. Then he began dreaming, while still awake, of the fine great vessel lying at the dock. Suppose his jolly Santa Claus man knew something about it! Suppose in some beautiful way he could manage to get aboard of her! It had been his pet dream for the last two years, — he was only about eight now, but ever since he had been a midget of six it had been his favourite dream imagining himself invited aboard a great sailing vessel. He never had been yet. Sailors had told him a good many things about them, and he fancied them full of strange, interesting places, and having all the mystery and enchantment of the sea clinging to every plank and spar. Some day, when he was ever so much older, his chance might come.

"What a thing it would be for Mr. Tony Winkers to hear of," he whispered to himself, "if such a happy day did come for me!" Then he thought again of his plan of relief, and hoped with all his little heart and soul it would only work, and the more he turned it over in his mind, the surer he felt that it was a good plan.

"Granny," he said in the morning, "isn't this the day when the overseer comes?"

He meant the clerk who acted for the "Overseers of the Poor," and brought granny a little money every month to buy food with.

"Yes, he comes to-day, Donny, sure."

"All right, may I go play in the court?"

"Yes, you can put on my ole sack. and play outside the door, if you won't go anywheres else."

"Well, I won't, granny."

Out went Donny, the plan of relief strong before his eyes. Before long the clerk appeared. He was young and important, and looked down at Donny as if he couldn't stop a moment, when the child began:

"Oh, please, mister, won't you give my granny a quarter more to-day? A bad boy tore my jacket to pieces, and we ain't got anythin' to mend it with. I'll go some errants for you if you will."

"No, little boy," said the young man, turning away, "we can't find food and clothes too. Your grandmother must look out for some other means of dressing you, and I don't want any errands done."

He ran quickly up the rickety steps, handed granny her money, then ran up a flight of stairs to give money to Mrs. Mellin, who, like granny, was too old and lame to go for it herself.

Great tears stood in Donny's eyes as the young man thus went about his business. He heard Mrs. Mellin's door shut, and knew that in another moment the young man would have gone away, and that door of hope be closed.

But alack and alas! Sometimes a smart-feeling young person flies around rather too quickly. Donny heard a sharp crack, and kind of slipping sound, and there over the narrow stairway came the smart clerk, bouncing, tumbling, scratching, and clutching for the old banister. Quick as thought the boy flew up the outside steps, and, planting his little body against the lower step of the long flight, saved the young man from rolling to the damp planking outside.

"Thank you, boy, you did that pretty cleverly for a small youngster," said the clerk as he got upon his feet. But — alack and alas again! — his snugly fitting coat was a sight to behold. It was of fuzzy, woolly stuff, very nice for a coolish day in October, but it was split at the shoulders, showing both shirt-sleeves, while the back was laid open nearly to the waist.

"Seems to me something's happened to my coat," he said, trying to peer around, with a very red face.

"It looks like my jacket," giggled Donny, who stood holding granny's old sack close about him to hide its shape.

"Well, now, see here, boy," began the crestfallen clerk, "you run up to Strong and Wolcott's with a note for me, and bring back a coat they'll send, and I'll give you half a dollar to get a new jacket."

"But granny won't let me," said Donny. "I'd be glad to if she would."

"Oh, well, run in and ask her," he said, impatiently.

"Don't you see the fix I'm in? And a pile of business waiting for my attention, too!"

Donny rushed into the house, begging to be allowed to do the errand. Granny came to the door. "My little boy ain't fit," she began.

"Oh, yes, he'll do very well," said the young man. "Just let him run up to the tailor's, and he may stop and get himself a jacket if he'll be quick about it. I'll give him this coat into the bargain; it will almost make an overcoat for him."

"Well, perhaps I might," began granny, and at the altered tone Donny darted away.

CHAPTER III.

CAPTAIN JACK SPLIFFINS.

It took the spry boy but a few moments to reach Strong and Wolcott's, to deliver the "overseer's" note, receive a bundle for that young man, then to be fitted to a good jacket which, selected from the last year's stock, was a much better one than Donny had ever owned before.

And in great glee the little fellow was soon on his way to the beloved roosting-place at the wharf, where, usually on a coil of rope, or perhaps on a box turned upside down, he would sit all day watching the boats or vessels unlade, keeping a sharp eye on the sailors going to and fro, or watching, with eyes that never tired of such sights, the tugs which would come to help the great vessels out to sea. Then, again, he would run over to the fishing-smacks that came up to another pier, and on these he was sometimes allowed to run about.

To-day it was his ambition to find out all he could

about the smart ship that had come up to the wharf two nights before. She surely did not arrive during the day. Never was sailor more anxious to know all about the bunk or berth he was to call his own for months to come than was Donny to know all he could about each vessel that arrived at the dock, what she brought, and what she was to carry to a foreign port. Where, the child got his fondness for the water, and every kind of craft that sailed its bosom, it would be hard to say. Very likely merely from having toddled to the docks as soon as he could toddle anywhere.

"Be careful and not fall in," granny warned one day, when Donny started for his usual pleasure-ground.

"Ho! I can swim," he called back; "and anyway, sailors doesn't let boys drown. I've fell in two or three times, and they always fished me out."

It was a very common thing for a good-natured fisherman to hand Donny a good plump fish from a keg; then, if only there was a bit of pork in granny's room, what a feast the strange pair would have, the old, old woman, and the little fair-faced, chattering child! If it was not exactly fit for a king, certain it is no king could have enjoyed it more.

As the lad's swift feet had borne him to the wharf

he saw that the large vessel was already unlading. "Ho! there's the stevedore and there's the supe'-cargo," he said, his practised little eyes taking in the whole state of affairs in a few quick glances.

"Jolly! I'm glad I'm here!" and planting himself on a soft, stray bale, he gave himself up to complete enjoyment of the busy scene.

"Jolly! she must 'a' come from awful far away! Lots and lots o' good things she's brought, for certain sure!"

Then he fell to wishing some one might come along that he could ask a few questions. All at once a man in a great loose purple jacket, baggy trousers, with a long braid down his back, passed close to where Donny was sitting. He did not need to be told that it was a Chinaman. He knew one at sight as quickly as any one. He never had spoken to one before, but as the man came near he plucked up courage and asked, while pointing to the vessel:

"Where does she come from? Can you tell?"

The man turned, with a wide, innocent smile. "She commee from Chinee, Chinee;" and he waved his hand in the direction of the other side of the sea.

"Wot did she bring?"

The man twisted his face, frowned, and smiled in his

effort to answer plainly. "She bringee tea, rice, silkee, nice dressee silkee, all velly nicee fan and mixy things."

Donny laughed, and the man laughed, too. "Wot's her name?" asked the boy.

"She have all velly nicee namee. Chinamans no tellee namee velly well. Ask sailor mans." Then the Chinaman moved gently away.

Donny strained his eyes to the utmost, hoping and longing to see some one who would look like the captain, but the unlading went briskly on, and no captain appeared. All at once he spied a large fishing-vessel lying quietly at another pier, where he must run into the street, and to the end of another wharf, if he wanted to find out about her, and see who was aboard.

"Guess I can't leave here yet," he muttered, and turning back, there, right before him, stood the Santa Claus man, the same pleasant smile twinkling in his eyes.

"So your folks let a little shaver like you run down to the wharf, hey?" he said, growing sober.

"Granny don't care," grinned Donny. "I always stays down here daytimes. Oh, please, wot's her name?" and he pointed to the vessel again.

"Hers? Oh, she's the *Nanetta Masters*. What do you think of her?"

"Isn't she a beauty, though!" As Donny said this, the quiet little grin that lighted up his face when anything pleased him made his countenance remind one of sunshine, sent the dimples into his cheeks, and made his bright little eyes grow long. The great man looked pleased, too, as he said:

"Aha, little mate, I see you are quite a judge of vessels. Know a good one when you see it, don't you? Well, now, that's *my* vessel, and, if you please, I happen to be Captain Jack Spliffins, at your service, sir."

Captain Spliffins placed a hand over his heart, and bent himself over with so low a bow it took a whole string of little giggles to show how greatly he pleased and amused the little fellow to whom he was speaking Then Donny took courage to say:

"I guess I'd like to see what there is inside of her, that great big ship."

"Well, some day you shall. You see there is no end of work going on just now. We're getting things off as fast as we can, and I am a man short. There is a large cargo, and things must be sent in several different directions."

"Please won't you tell me all about her?" urged Donny, with an eager air. "A Chinaman told me she come from Chiny, and brought lots o' fine things, but he couldn't talk very plain, and I ruther hear 'bout a ship than anythin' else there is."

"Well, now, I think a lad of your size that wants to know where a vessel has been, what her cargo is, and all about her, ought to have some attention. I can't spend but about two minutes now, but, in a word, the *Nanetta Masters* has been to China since she sailed from New York last, and has brought back chests of tea, also rice, silks, painted porcelains, preserves, and a large stock of fancy things in carved ivory and woods. There! The men are beckoning to me; the captain is wanted. Good day, little mate, don't forget the captain promised you should go aboard the ship some day." And, with a seaman's swift salute, the captain hurried away.

Forget it! Why, it seemed to Donny that nothing Tony Winkers or any other bad boy on earth could do would trouble him the least bit in the world now. "Unless he tears me all to pieces," put in the boy, "so there wasn't clothes enough left to run about in." But, even in that case, there came a kind of delightful feeling that if anything dreadful did happen, through Tony or one of his kind, word could somehow be sent to Captain Jack Spliffins of the *Nanetta Masters*, "and he's jus' the man that would come if I sent for him to," Donny whispered, with his satisfied little grin.

Every one who had anything to do with the vessel was far too busy to pay any more attention to a small boy on the landing, so Donny thought he had better run over to the fishing-boat, and see what there might be to pick up or to amuse him there.

He started away slowly, looking back every moment or two at the ship that he already hated to lose sight of; but at the pier where the fishermen most often landed, he was pleased to see Sam Dickson was one of the men just in from a fishing cruise.

Any child who spends most of the time in one or two particular places, as Donny did, is sure to pick up acquaintances of a certain kind. Sam Dickson was a good-hearted, industrious man, who liked children, and always had a cheerful word for this child, whose face was familiar to many of the fishermen and those employed about the docks.

"When did you get in, Sam?" asked the child, with the easy, friendly manner that Sam liked.

"We landed last night, little boy, and a good big haul we've had of it, too."

"Been unloading?" The question was asked in a businesslike way.

"Ain't goin' to unload ourselves, Mr. Donny. We've sold ev'ry blessed fish outright, — barrin' a few we take home, — sold the whole 'catch' at wholesale to some fish dealers, so they're to do the whole business o' unloadin' and cartin' away. You hold on, and I'll give you a big bundle to carry home."

"Mayn't I come on to her, Sam?"

"Well, I guess you better not. The place is wet and slippery as can be. We don't rush things, when we unship, the way fellows does that takes a contract. Sakes! How they pounded and slashed about! But there's a bar'l yonder that has some awful nice, sweet swimmers in it, and if I can manage without breaking my neck, I'll give you a bite for supper, and 'nuff for breakfast, too."

"Did you make a nice trip, Sam."

"Fine, so fur as the business went, but I'm most tired of fishing-trips, and I don't just relish this selling the lot, and handing over things by the whole job. I'm done fishing for the present, but I can't abide bein' idle. I don't know where I'll be goin' for work next. I wish I knew whereabouts to look for it."

"I'll tell you where you can get work right away, Sam;" and Donny looked sober, and felt a little important that he could help Sam so easily. "There's a great sailing vessel over to Holland Wharf, and she's just arrived from Chiny."

Donny had to laugh at his own off-hand speech, but he went on: "My sakes, Sam! she's jus' cram full o' tea and silk and rice, and — oh! all sorts o' Chiny things. And I guess if ever you see a cap'n in your life as *is* a cap'n, it's Cap'n Jack Spliffins!"

"Captain Spliffins," said Sam, with a thoughtful air; "what, a man that's mos' as big round as he is high, and that rolls about like a porpo's' when he walks?"

"Yes, but he's dretful nice, Sam."

"Yes, I expect so," said Sam. "I remember when he was in port before. I heard tell that he was fine to sail with, but that 'twas hard gettin' a chance with him. The crew mostly doesn't change much. But what about that's havin' anythin' to do with my gettin' a job?"

"Well, he's a hand short," said Donny. "He tole me so himself to-day. Now you oughter go right over to Holland Wharf, and see Cap'n Spliffins. I wisht I was big 'nuff to be a hand!"

"Well, I think p'r'aps I'll take your advice, Donny boy, but wait till I treat you."

He disappeared, and was gone some little time. When he came in sight again he had a large newspaper bundle in his hands. "There, that's a pretty bulky cargo for a craft o' your size," he said, "but I'll carry it a piece for you, then you better run right home with it, and I'll go see your Captain Spliffins."

"Oh, and I'm goin' aboard the *Nanetta Masters* myself some day," said Donny, proudly; "the cap'n promised me I should."

"All right, you'll have a fine time when you do," Sam replied with a nod.

CHAPTER IV.

THE NANETTA MASTERS.

Donny went skipping home, stopping every little while to push the heavy bundle further into his arms with one knee. He was so happy and contented that he gave never a thought to any possible trouble or accident. He did not see the wicked little eyes of Tony Winkers watching him as he capered along, nor hear the naughty boy running softly up behind.

The first thing he knew there was a quick push, a grab, and his bundle was thrown to the ground. Sam Dickson had tied it up so snugly that the fish did not fall out, but Tony began scratching and scrambling, trying to push Donny aside so he could catch up the package and make off with it. But Donny was no little coward, to stand by and see the larger boy steal his bundle without using his hands in trying to save it. No sooner did he understand what had happened than he began crying out to Tony to let alone, and he struggled hard to push him away.

But the louder Donny cried, the louder Tony mocked him, and the scuffle went on until both were making such a noise that a policeman came running around the corner, and caught hold of both boys as they fought over the bundle lying on the sidewalk.

"Well, what's all this hullabaloo?" said the strong man, taking each boy by the collar, and jerking him up before him. "Oh, a pretty kettle of fish!" he exclaimed, as the strong smell reached him, and the end of a fish's tail was seen sticking through the paper.

"It's — it's — my — fish! that Sam Dickson give me," sobbed Donny.

"'Tain't either!" cried Tony, "it's mine; he was tryin' to rob me."

"Oh, what a story!" began Donny.

"Now, now!" said the policeman, "one of you kids is a precious rogue, and it's my business to find out which one of you 'tis. It won't take me long. But one or the other of you needs to be marched off to the station-house, and taught decent manners."

At that Donny began crying, at the same time he tried to tell the policeman the truth. This gave Tony a chance to make up a story of his own.

"That great baby lives with his granny," he began, "and I wor carryin' home that bundle when he run up, and tried to snatch it away. 'Tain't no great crime, anyway," Tony added, as it suddenly came into his mind to wonder what would be done to the boy which was found to be guilty.

"Hi! what's the matter here?" said an amused voice, as a young man stopped a moment before the policeman and the two urchins. A glance showed Donny that it was the "overseer," as he called him, and very glad he was to make a plea that he thought might help him.

"Oh, please," he said, "won't you tell this police as I'm granny Hilborn's boy, and as I ain't a thief? I was runnin' home with some fish Sam Dickson give me, when Tony Winkers rushed up, and tried to snatch it away, then tole the police a story."

The young man went a little closer to Master Tony, who gave a swift glance, as if thinking of running away. "You'd better keep tight hold of this young rascal," he said.

At that Tony did dart aside, but the policeman's strong clutch tightened on his collar, and held him fast. "Perhaps this is the same chap who tore your jacket to threads just for sport?" said the "overseer," looking at Donny.

"Yes, it is," said the trembling boy, "but I don't

want nothin' dretful done to Tony," for the child's eyes had grown large with a kind of terror as he saw that hard grasp holding Tony so firmly.

"We sha'n't eat him up," said the policeman, with a smile that Donny thought was a very pleasant one, "nor we sha'n't let him eat you up, fish and all, either, so come on, boy."

Tony, coward as he was, began crying and sobbing as the policeman started off with him, telling Donny to pick up his fish, and run home. The young man had walked away, and Donny was too frightened and troubled to think to thank him. But the boy's kind little heart could not stand the sound of Tony's distress, and after gathering up his bundle he ran after the policeman.

"Oh, please, Mr. Police, do let Tony go!" he cried. "He won't be plaguing me any more, and I don't want him put in prison."

"We sha'n't put him in prison, my boy," said the tall man, "but he must come up to the station-house, and explain why he wants to torment a boy that is littler than he. He spoiled some of your clothing, and grabbed your fish, and told me a lie; now he must give his reasons for it, that's all. Run home and get your supper. Mr. Tony will probably be on the street to-morrow, and *probably* he will let smaller boys alone."

There was no more to be said, and Donny turned away with the sound of Tony's blubbering still in his ears.

"I don't b'lieve a man with such a pleasant-looking smile will do anythin' very dretful," he thought; still, it was a dreadful thing to the boy's mind to be marched off by a great towering policeman, with his hand holding so tight to a boy he could not possibly wriggle away.

Donny was learning what it is that gives a boy or a man a feeling of awe, when he sees the blue coat and brass buttons of a policeman. Or what it is that makes people peep time and again at the glittering bayonets of a company of soldiers, and feel there is something of power about them it wouldn't do to trifle with. It is because back of the shining buttons and glittering bayonets lies *the law!* And oh, the law is a mighty power, a very mighty power indeed! A very much dreaded power when even a child dares to break it. But then, it is what protects us, keeps us in safety, and guards us, so it is a very blessed thing, after all.

There was so much to tell granny when Donny reached Sunrise Court, that his little tongue ran as

"'OH, PLEASE, MR. POLICE, DO LET TONY GO!' HE CRIED."

fast as it could. But granny did not appear to pay much attention to what he said. She moved slowly about, getting ready to cook some of the nice fish the boy had brought, but she seemed stupid, and Donny wondered if she was very tired and sleepy, it took her so long to get things out. Granny didn't usually move about in that way. She was old and rather deaf, but she had been wide awake, and made a chowder almost as quickly as anybody. To-night she poked about as if it was hard to move.

"Come," she said, after what Donny thought was a long, long time, "take the purse, and go for a three-cent loaf. We'll be havin' supper right away; it's ready now."

That was another strange thing. Granny never told him to "take the purse." When she sent him on an errand she took a piece of money out and handed him, but he was never trusted with the purse. He knew just where she kept it, at the bottom of an old crockery sugar-bowl, and that she was careful to keep it on a high shelf in the tiny closet. But Donny did as he was told, got up on a wooden chair, reached up and got the old worn pocketbook, and was very careful when he paid for the bread not to drop out a few bits of soiled paper in one of the parts.

Donny wished granny would say something about Tony, and that she was glad he did not get away with their supper, but she did not feel like talking, and went to bed early, so Donny had to go too, and he must have been pretty tired, for he soon was fast asleep, and dreamed of seeing the "overseer" parading down the court in a policeman's coat and helmet, when all at once he turned into a fish, and the boy woke himself up, he was laughing so hard.

The next morning it was cool and clear. Granny was a little brighter, there was plenty of fish for breakfast, and in his good, stout jacket Donny started for the wharf in great spirits. He thought of Tony, but in the fresh morning light things look brighter than they do at dusk or in the dark; the policeman had said Tony would probably be on the street in the morning, so there was no use in worrying.

At the wharf all was bustle and clatter, and, to his great delight, Donny saw Sam Dickson hurrying to and fro. Sam had found work, and no mistake. "I got him that job, if I am little," Donny muttered, with his little satisfied smile; "now p'r'aps Sam could get me on board if he was a-mind to."

He waited a long time, for it was a busy hour, but at last Sam passed so near his perch that Donny hailed him. "Oh, Sam," he cried, "say, can't I go on board somewhere, and jus' watch the men at work? I'll curl up in a corner, and not make a sound, but it would be such fun, I want to dretful, Sam! If you ask the cap'n, I know he'll let me; please won't you, Sam?"

The man laughed at the boy, he was so much in earnest. "Well, now, the tide'll be down more in another hour or two," he said. "She's ridin' well aloft this minute, is the *Nanetta*, and we had to come ashore by the ship's ladder. We manage with a gang-plank at low tide when we unlade, and the deck's a solid mass with what'll have to come off early this afternoon at the fall o' the tide. P'r'aps now you better wait."

"Ho! I ain't afraid o' the ladder," said Donny, glancing at the straight ropes with cross rope bars swaying at the side of the great vessel. "Jus' you ask cap'n,— oh, here he is now!" And Donny made a dive as the rolling figure of Captain Spliffins hove in sight.

"Aha! Just as lively as ever, I see," sung out the merry shipmaster. "Well, now, how did we pass the night, I wonder, and is it all right with our little mate to-day?"

Donny giggled in the quiet, amused way that had attracted the captain from the first, then begged leave to go aboard the *Nanetta Masters* under Sam Dickson's care.

"Ah, yes, Mr. Dickson came to me with your letters of advice," said the captain, and although Donny had no idea what "letters of advice" meant, he imagined it was only said in fun, for Sam Dickson laughed outright, and the captain's eyes twinkled. "The vessel isn't just pretty to go aboard of now," he went on. "Everything is in disorder, the cargo partly unshipped, and there's no end of scurrying to and fro, fore and aft; you might wish yourself out of such confusion."

"No, I shouldn't, and if I could only get aboard," pleaded Donny, "I wouldn't make a bit o' trouble."

"Well, well, if Mr. Dickson is a-mind to see you safely on and off, I like to let little folks have all the fun they can. So if you'll promise not to go aloft, nor play with the anchor, go on; you have my permission; but stay right on deck, don't attempt to go below anywhere."

So a very happy little boy prepared to clutch at the man-ropes, and went dancing to the great vessel's side. "Now," said Sam, "cling close to the ropes, and mind what I tell you: go steadily up, and *don't look down.*

Just keep your eyes before you, and you'll be all right. Wait a bit till I whistle to a man on deck to help you over the side. I'll come behind, but never mind me."

Sam gave a shrill whistle, and a man with a kind of fatigue cap on peered over the vessel.

"Help this weasel aboard, will you, please?" shouted Sam, and the next moment Donny was going carefully, hand over hand, up the ship's side. He went bravely on until a strong hand clutched his wrist, and the next instant he had fairly boarded the *Nanetta Masters*, and was standing on deck, the very picture of boyish satisfaction.

"Now, what did he say his little name was?" asked the man, putting one hand back of his ear, and looking Donny in the face, with a mischievous smile.

"I'm Donny Hilborn," said the boy, with the customary quiet grin, and thinking the pleasant man must be a sailor, although he seemed higher up than most of the other sailors about, who wore flat cloth caps with ribbon streamers at the back.

"This little chap is to be tucked in some corner where he can see all that's going on, and yet be out o' the way," explained Sam. "Captain said as he might come aboard, and so here he is."

"Well, seeing he climbed for it pretty bravely, I don't see but we'll have to give the little scamp a berth somewhere," said the man. "Just you come here, little friend," and leading Donny to an immense coil of rope, he threw over it a rubber coat with the lining uppermost. "Now, sir, sit you there, and see all you can," he said, "and by and by I'll bring you a biscuit."

Yet, with all his easy, friendly manner, there was an air of command about this seaman that made Donny think he seemed more like the captain than any one else.

The rope was piled so high that the boy could not only see across the crowded deck, but he could also gaze along the wharf, which looked very far down. He wanted no further attention. Perfectly happy, in the place of his long cherished dreams, he feasted his eyes one moment on the busy scene on deck; the next he watched with sweet content the hurrying figures beneath him on the wharf. All at once a grin of real delight overspread his face.

"Oh, goody! goody!" he said, in an undertone, "there's Tony! He isn't shut up anywheres. I can't see his face, but I'd know the queer way he runs, soon as I saw him."

Every day after that, while the unlading was going on, Sam Dickson was allowed by the indulgent captain to take Donny on board, and the child would find some

DONNY ON DECK.

perch on deck where he straightway was thankful to stay until dark. One day Captain Spliffins came close to the boy, who knew right away, by the twinkling of the captain's merry eyes, that something pleasant was coming.

"See here, little mate," he said, " we are going to be all quiet and in good order around this vessel in a few days, then, — whisper!" He came closer, put his hand side of his mouth, and said, in a loud whisper, " You're going to have a little party on board!"

CHAPTER V.

THE PARTY ABOARD SHIP.

It seemed to Donny that the whole world had become different, in a way, since the *Nanetta Masters* had anchored at Holland Wharf, with her kind, child-loving master, Captain Jack Spliffins, in command.

There hadn't been very much that was bright in his little life, that Donny could remember; yet the child scarcely knew it, because his sunny little temper had done so much for him that, as long as he was free to run to the water's side, and use his eyes and limbs, he wanted nothing better.

But lately granny had changed. There were days when she kept him indoors from morning till night, helping her cook, and put to rights the two poor little rooms that she called "the house." Then there were many errands to be done of various kinds. These shut-in days were the greatest trials of the boy's life, but granny would keep reminding him that she was getting very old, and that if anything happened to her there was no knowing what would become of him; she guessed he would have to be a "bound-boy."

That was her old-fashioned idea, and one day Donny said to Sam Dickson, "What is it to be a bound-boy, Sam?"

"Mostly they don't have them much now," Sam replied, "but they used to take boys as hadn't any father nor mother, and 'bind them over,' as 'twas called, to a farmer, or a tinker, or wot not, and then 'twas the same as if the man had bought the boy, and my! wouldn't that shaver have to work!"

"And couldn't he go to the wharf at all?" asked Donny, his eyes stretching wide at the idea.

"Wharf! Well, I guess not!" said Sam, with a knowing laugh. "Gen'rally 'twas to the country the boy would go, where there ain't any such thing as a wharf for miles and miles. You'd have to go on the railroad to get to one. And a bound-boy has to work all day long, and only gets his food and clothes for pay. Has to stay, too, until he's a grown-up young man."

The picture of a bound-boy was not soon to fade out of Donny's mind. He would think of it at night just as soon as his head touched the pillow. And if he happened to forget it for a little while, granny would speak of it again, and then the picture would come back, looking ten times worse than before. For if there was one thing in the world certain to Donny's mind, it was that he never, never could live without a sight of the water and the ships he loved with all his heart; and to be miles and miles away from a wharf, why, there could be no darker thought than that to him.

But now, all visions of a bound-boy, of Tony Winkers, and everything else unpleasant was driven away, just as if Captain Spliffins had taken a broom called "sunshine," and swept away everything dark and trying before it, in sending that magic whisper into the boy's ear, of a little party aboard the *Nanetta Masters*.

What did he really mean? Well, whatever he meant, it was going to be something perfectly delightful, there could be no doubt of that. Perhaps the captain was going to invite a number of small friends he had picked up to a little feast with himself and the mates. But, no. "He said, '*you* are goin' to have a little party on board,'" Donny said to himself, in thinking it over for the twentieth time, "and that must 'a' meant I was to have consid'rable to do with it."

The next day, as the boy went gliding along his beloved wharf, the captain met him face to face.

"Now, my boy," he began, — "and, by the way, what is your name, I wonder?"

"Folks all call me 'Donny.' But granny told me once as my name was Donald, so it's Donald Hilborn."

"Well, now, that is a fine name, I think," said the captain, who sometimes spoke so soberly that Donny began to think there appeared to be two Captain Spliffins's, one a very kind but sober man, and the other a man who was only kind and jolly way through.

"I think I had rather call you Donald," he went on, "because it sounds more manly to give a boy a good, sensible name; but we'll have lots of sport for all that, won't we, Donald? Now, to-morrow afternoon, at two o'clock, near the fall of the tide, I want you should come with three or four of your little friends, and we'll show you over the *Nanetta Masters* pretty thoroughly. My mate, Mr. Tom Hallers, has got pretty well acquainted with the little chap who has perched on deck, and seen that the unlading went on all right. But some of my friends on shipboard you have never seen yet, nor anything of the good ship herself, except just the deck, and only one part of that, there has been so much lying all around. To-morrow it will be all spick and span:

"Don't be late, it grows dark early these nights; and Mr. Hallers, my mate, who gives biscuits to small boys every chance he sees, if he happens to fancy them, will help show the little folks aboard, and see that things are shipshape in other parts of the vessel. You see, I don't have time to do so very much good in this big, round world, but I like, after landing, to do something to make some one happy. It is pleasant to think of afterwards. Every one who possibly can ought to do something to make others happy."

Donny's face, which had been full of smiles, all at once grew quite sober.

"What made the sun go in, I should like to know?" said the captain.

The boy was bright enough to understand that it was his sober look his friend had noticed.

He began slowly in reply, "I ain't got any clothes but just these. Granny's poor, and Tom Smart's poor, so if I should ask Tom—" the boy stopped, scarcely knowing just how to go on.

"Donald," said the captain, putting his head to one side, and speaking so every word was clear and simple, "I want you always to remember that it isn't clothes that make the man or the boy. Why, I saw a man once, dressed in the finest clothes there are, with a ring on his finger, a splendid gold watch in his pocket, and money in his purse; but he was on his way to prison for having cheated other men. Which would you rather be, my boy, that fine peacock of a man in the finest of clothing, or Mr. Donald Hilborn, a wharf-bird, with a clean heart, and little trousers that are rather worn? Eh, my boy?"

"I'd ruther be me," said Donny, grinning sublimely.

"Yes, I guess you had. So no matter how your little mates are dressed to-morrow, I sha'n't mind that at all. All children can have clean faces and hands, and can comb their hair; further than that no one need worry. There's only one thing I like better than to see little people happy, and that is to know they're good. Now, then, sermon's all through; to-morrow, at two by the clock, is the time set; don't forget, little mate."

Then the captain was gone, and Donny felt more full of business than he ever had before in his life.

Whom to invite? Tom Smart for one, who lived in the next row of houses, and was always willing to help Donny about an errand when he wanted him to. Then there was a lame boy in a tenement opposite the court, whose father left him alone all day, except Sundays, to amuse himself with the sparrows, and the carts going by, or anything else to be seen from the window.

"If I help Billy Bean, like his father does Sundays, and he takes his cane 'long, I can get him to the wharf all right," murmured Donny; "then the sailors will help him aboard, and, my! what a time it'll be for Billy! That makes two, and cap'n said three or four." He rubbed his hands joyously, and went on :

"Guess I better ask Sally Jackman. Nothin' was said 'bout girls, but Sally's been orful sick, and now she's jus' pokin' out for a little walk ev'ry day. I know the water air will do Sally good, and won't her eyes stick out to get an invite on a ship like that! That's three. Now for one more, that'll make five o' us in all, jus' a nice little party."

Then something came into Donny's mind at which the little fellow looked very sober indeed. "Oh, I don't want to," he said. He thought and thought, kicking a stone before him with his toe as he went slowly along. Then he said, still lower, "P'r'aps I oughter." Then, in a brighter tone, "P'r'aps it might make him a betterer boy."

Ah! he was thinking of Tony Winkers, and it wasn't pleasant to think of him, not pleasant at all. But it was only a moment before the bright little face cleared entirely. "I guess I better," he said. "If 'twas me I'd feel orful to see other boys goin' on a big vessel, and me lef' out." That settled it.

Three who were invited to Donny's party accepted the invitation with delight. It was far too joyful a thing to mince matters. The boy told each one that all the dressing up they need think of would just be to have "clean faces and hands, and hair combed." The truth was, not one of the three had ever been invited to any kind of a party before.

The next morning Donny set out to find Tony Winkers, the only guest not yet invited. "Funny I haven't seen Tony anywheres yesterday nor day before," Donny thought, as he trudged along. "Hate to go down by his house, but mean to, anyway."

Not far from Tony's house, which was a much better one than where Donny lived, the boy came skulking along, and on seeing who was coming he called out, crossly:

"P'r'aps you'd better brought a cop along to 'rest me, p'r'aps you had! I bet next time there's a row 'twon't be me gets run to the station-house, and kep' all night!"

"Oh, say, Tony," cried Donny, wisely taking no notice of Tony's foolish little speech, "I'm going to have a party this afternoon on the *Nanetta Masters*, down to Holland Wharf, and I come to ask you to go. And we must only have 'clean faces and hands, and hair combed.' We must meet at Sunrise Court, ten minutes o' two. There's goin' to be Tom Smart, Billy Bean, and Sally Jackman, and you and me."

Donny talked fast, so as to tell the whole story before Tony could reply, and only added, "We'll all go together; won't it be nice?"

"No, I don't want to go to any party o' yourn."

"All right, then, I'll ask Davy Trotmore instead;" and feeling much relieved, Donny turned away. But he had not got rid of Master Tony Winkers quite so easily.

"I say," cried the boy, running after Donny, "who said to invite me?"

"No one said to, only Captain Spliffins tole me yes'day I might have a little party on shipboard, and I was to ask three or four friends to come. So I thought you would like to see the big ship, and I'd ask you; but Davy Trotmore will go, I know, so I guess you better not, Tony."

"You're a great plum, you are! Ask a fellow somewheres, then tell 'im he better not come!" sneered Tony.

"Because you said you didn't want to," called out Donny, as he ran away.

He was glad to leave the disagreeable boy, and yet feel he had given him a chance to make one of the party had he wanted to. "But he said right out he didn't want to go," Donny thought, as he ran to see Davy Trotmore. "Dear me!" he whispered, "I must hurry up. It'll be two o'clock first thing I know!" It was then about half-past nine in the morning.

As Davy was pleased as could be at Donny's errand, and could easily find the convenient dress suit of "clean face and hands, and hair combed," it was one of the happiest of groups that met at Sunrise Court that October afternoon. Granny Hilborn was still half stupid a good deal of the time, but made no objection to Donny's going where he pleased.

Tom Smart, with his hair plastered as close to his head as soap and water could stick it, was an awkward boy, some older than Donny, but by no means a bad-looking lad as he stood at the entrance of Sunrise Court, all ready for the party to start. Billy Bean looked neatly enough as, leaning on his cane with one hand, he linked the other arm in Donny's to be piloted along. Sally Jackman, pale as a little ghost after her long sickness, was a pitiful little object in her patched gown, her mouth stretched wide with pleasure at thought of what was before her. Davy Trotmore, an eager-looking child, was all impatience to be on the way.

"Come, now it's time to go," said Donny. At that moment Tony Winkers appeared, neither with very clean hands or a neat-looking head.

"Guess I've jus' as good a right to go on the *Masters* boat as any o' the rest o' you," he said, jauntily, as he joined the group. "Come on, I won't keep you waitin'."

CHAPTER VI.

THE PARTY ABOARD SHIP — CONTINUED.

Donny did not know what to say or do about Tony. He wished the boy would go away, but scarcely dared ask him to. The captain had said ask three or four friends, and what would he think to see five besides Donny?

"He won't care," thought the boy, "but I do;" for there was something in Donny's nature that was finer and more delicate than any one would have looked for in a little street boy living at Sunrise Court. But then there *are* fine natures to be found, now and then, where one would least expect to find them.

At Holland Wharf, a wide gang-plank was slanting from the deck of the vessel to the wharf, and Mr. Hallers was standing at the end to show the children up. Midway up stood Sam Dickson, and to him, while a sailor on deck was putting the plank in a little firmer position, Donny told of the fix in which Tony Winkers had placed him.

"Oh, that'll be all right," said Sam. "Captain won't count who's come and who hasn't."

But just then, as lame Billy Bean was being led up the slanting way by Mr. Hallers, who had taken him in charge, Tony Winkers pushed by him to be the next one to reach the deck after Donny, who had been told he had better go aboard first of all.

"See here," said Sam Dickson, sternly, "you just walk back, young Winkers, and wait till Billy Bean and that frail little girl have been shown up, will you? Where's your manners? And why didn't you comb your hair decent before you started?"

"'Cause I didn't want to," growled Tony, "and you ain't got no call to talk 'bout my hair."

But he turned sulkily back, and as Mr. Hallers handed Billy over to Sam to be helped up the last half of the way, the mate, who had heard Tony's reply to Sam Dickson, said, shortly, "You can take yourself home, young man, about as fast as you can travel! Captain Spliffins wouldn't have any such voice nor any such looking a head aboard his vessel. You might exactly as well have me send you kiting as the captain, for he'd be sure to the moment he set eyes on you."

The severe look, big frame, and determined voice scared the cowardly Tony, who went very quickly off the plank, muttering, "Didn't want to go, anyway, and told him so. only he coaxed me;" but no notice was taken of his mumbling, and the little party were all soon on board. Then Sam Dickson went up to Donny, as he stood a little apart from the others, and said, softly:

"Tony Winkers thought best to make a few pert remarks, and Mr. Hallers sent him home hummin'. You won't have any further trouble with him to-day."

As Mr. Hallers was the kind-hearted man "who gives biscuits to small boys every chance he gets," according to Captain Spliffins, the comforting thought shot through Donny's mind, that if such a good man had sent Tony away, he surely deserved to go.

Then the pleasure that followed was so new and strange, that each child forgot everything except the enjoyment of the moment. They looked about on deck for a while, wondering at the size and quantity of ropes and "iron things" they saw.

"Guess you better peep into the fo'c's'l first," said Mr. Hallers, and the five little people went to the upper deck, "for'ard," as the sailors called it, and looked at the queer, narrow rooms, with the wooden beds built close against the wall. They were clean and neat as could be, and to these children looked as if they might be very comfortable when the weather was not too rough. They visited the galley or cook-room, and saw Loo Sing, the Chinaman to whom Donny had spoken on the wharf. Rows and rows of tin plates, tin mugs, tea-pots, coffee-pots, all kinds of tin dishes, were ranged around, while a great cook-stove made up a kind of pleasant dream of good things that came from oven, stew-pan, and soup-kettle.

Then they went to the quarter-deck, the place where the ship-master is thought to walk as king, "but as to that," said Mr. Hallers, "he is king, boss, and grand commander of vessel, crew, and everything aboard when we are on the sea. It is quite a thing to walk the quarter-deck as captain of a fine ship. But careful, now! Here we go down the companionway to the cabin. This is the ship's parlour, reading-room, and dining-room for captain and mate. A right fine place we call it, too."

The children went gingerly over the narrow stairs, admiring the rows of bright brass nails at the sides; but the next moment they opened wide their eyes in surprise, for such a room as they found themselves in!

The middle of the floor, in the long, cheerful place, was covered with a thick, soft rug. In one corner was a bookcase built into the wall, with high, curious railings holding the books safely in place. In the centre was a large table covered with a handsome cloth held in place by brass clamps, and on it was a small bookrack, and a case with a rim around it, holding pencils and pens.

The children perhaps did not notice that everything had rather a stiff, prim look. A lounge was placed against the wall on one side of the room, and a few large, comfortable-looking chairs stood here and there. A fine large chair that could be twirled around — what is called a revolving chair — stood close by the table, and another table, very shining and polished, with a railing around the edge, and with railings on different places about it on the surface, was at the end of the cabin nearest the door or entrance.

But it was, after all, the living creatures in the roomy place that most delighted the youthful visitors. In a strong cage securely fastened to the cabin's side, was a great bird of green and gold with a long white bill, that eyed the children keenly as they stood around, scarcely knowing what to look at first. Then two dear little objects, with beautiful feathers, chipped and chirped and huddled close to each other as if half afraid of the new guests. In still a third cage, some yellow birds hopped about, now and then trilling a little song.

Perched on a kind of shelf in another corner, with a chain about his neck, was a little monkey, who, quick as a flash, jumped to Donny's shoulder, grabbed his cap out of his hand, jumped back to his shelf chattering and scolding, then coolly put the cap under him, and sat down on it.

"You saucy little tyke!" said Mr. Hallers, while the children shouted with laughter.

"Ha! ha! ha!" screamed the bird with the feathers of green and gold. "Oh, what a fright! What a fright! Put 'im out! Put 'im out!"

At this, the children gazed open-mouthed at the sober-looking bird. "What is it? What is it?" asked Sally Jackman, who had not spoken before since coming aboard.

"Now, sissy, you look tired," said Mr. Hallers; "sit you down on the lounge there, and you, Billy boy," he added, turning to Billy Bean, leaning partly on his cane and partly on the table, "sit right down side of her; the rest of you can sit where you please while I tell you a thing or two. This is the captain's family here, all the family he has. That spry fellow, Jocko, over there, is a little African monkey. He was caught in a rich tangle-wood where all sorts of tropical — that means hot weather or hot climate — things grow in great abundance. I can only take time to tell you now that the mischievous little wretch has to be kept with a chain about the length of the cabin around him, except when the captain is about, then he minds what is told him, and slips his chain awhile.

"That gay girl in yonder cage is a parrot captain got in Australia, lying down between the South Pacific and the Indian Oceans. She used to screech so she could be heard almost from stream to stream; but that we broke up, now she jabbers and laughs more like a human being, and you'd just be surprised at the way she can talk. The sailors have had lots of fun with Polly, and she'd say things to amaze you.

"Those two cunning little chatterers are paroquets; they came from Sydney, in Australia, too, and those cockatoos with the high crowns were a present from another sea-captain. In that big cage are canary birds, and once in a while they sing fit to stun you.

"Now perhaps you notice things have a kind of set look, just as if they were all placed right on the square. If you look a little sharp, you will see that everything is screwed tight to the floor or the wall."

"What is that for?" asked Davy Trotmore, looking around.

"What do you think, little mate?" asked Mr. Hallers, looking at Donny.

"I think," began Donny, with his usual quiet little grin, "it is 'cause, when the ship's a-goin', things would tumble 'bout everywheres, 'les' they was fastened to somethin'."

Davy said, "Oh, yes," as though he might have thought of that.

"That is just exactly the reason," said Mr. Tom Hallers, nodding his head at Donny. "Chairs, tables, cages, everything, would dance every which way, unless the screws kept them in place."

"That's a yarn! That's a yarn! Pitch 'im out! Pitch 'im out!" croaked Polly, and off went the little folks into roars of laughter at the sober, saucy bird.

"Now, here is the captain's room, and mine just beyond," said Mr. Hallers, leading to some home-like little rooms out from the cabin. "We call them state-rooms. And then just across from the cabin, in this direction, is the ship's pantry." He entered a room larger than either of granny Hilborn's, where, hanging in cases and placed in closets so they could not move, were finer dishes than any child of the company had ever seen before. There was also a sweet smell as of oranges and other things, cake perhaps, that were stored away in some of the neat drawers.

"Let's go aft for a bit," said the mate; "then you shall go below, and by that time captain'll be back. He had to go ashore on important business. We're going to take in cargo soon; then all will be bustle again."

He went up and "aft," showed them the clock in the coop near the wheel, and told how, at certain hours, the man struck "four bells" and "eight bells," which was the signal for changing the watch. The crew, he said, was divided into two watches, each serving for four hours; there is also the "dog-watch" of two hours from four to six in the afternoon, which changes the men. "When the bells strike," he said, "it calls to the sailors 'for'ard' in their bunks, 'Come, turn out! Your time has come!'"

The happy little crowd followed the mate about, peeped down the hatchways, which were openings for getting "'tween decks," and at last they went down and peeped into the "hold," the great place at the bottom of the vessel running from end to end. Poor little Sally Jackman trembled like a leaf, as, keeping tight hold of Mr. Hallers's hand, she went down a few steps of the ladder-like stairs, and looked around the deep, dark, long, wide place. Oh, she was so glad to get up again where the light was! But the boys thought it great sport to look across the "great hole," as Billy Bean called it, and, with Mr. Hallers's help, he got a good, long view of it.

"That's where the chief part of the cargo goes in," said the mate. "But hark! I hear the captain's voice; now let's back to the cabin and meet him." He led the way to the cabin, where, at the entrance, stood Captain Jack, his merry eyes twinkling like stars at sight of his poor little guests.

"Well, how are you all, and have your little friends been enjoying themselves?" he asked, looking at Donny; "and has Mr. Hallers been good to you?" Then, without waiting for an answer, he looked around and said, "Aha! I see Mr. Loo Sing has been up to his old habit of setting a table; come, let's see if he has anything here that any of us like."

Such a pretty spread! Neither Donny Hilborn, Tom Smart, Billy Bean, Sally Jackman, or Davy Trotmore knew the names of some of the nice things, or had ever seen them.

"And now, are we all as hungry as bears?" asked the captain, as he seated them around. "That's good, as we must eat all we can, seeing Mr. Loo has done his best."

First there were little sandwiches, with bread so soft,

and meat chopped so fine, they slipped down the little throats as if they melted away. Then there were cakes filled with "plums," as the sailors call raisins, and with a soft, delicious frosting on top, that was white, and with pink sugar sand sprinkled over it. Sally Jackman thought they looked like lovely pictures. Next came preserves the captain called "mangoes." "They're little apples we get preserved in India," the captain explained; "and these green things are fresh figs, from India, too. Now save room for nuts and plums. These plums"—great clusters of raisins—"came from Spain. The bunches of fine, large Spanish grapes are dried in the sun, and then packed and sold as raisins. Those oranges are from Spain, too; you shall each have one to carry home. These soft-shelled almonds are from the West Indies, and that candied ginger from Canton, in China."

The little people feasted royally for an hour. Loo Sing slipped the rind from the oranges, and laid them in sections on little side plates, so that each guest could eat his or her orange easily, then he went around smiling serenely, and laid a package at each plate. In each package was a great orange, some figs, nuts, and raisins done up in a large, showy napkin of Chinese paper. These were to be taken home.

After leaving the table the little company ran about the cabin as they pleased. The captain unchained little Jocko, who at once climbed to his shoulder and kept patting his cheek. Polly sang out, "Oh, dear! dear! how-dy-do! how-dy-do! Glad you're back, Captain Jack! glad you're back!" Then she croaked in so dismal a tone it made the children laugh afresh: "Poll's dretful hungry! dretful hungry! Here we go down! down! down! Ha! ha! ha!" she screamed, changing her tone, and mocking the children's laughter, and the louder they laughed the louder Polly screamed, "Ha! ha! ha!" until the paroquets and cockatoos chattered noisily, Jocko scolded, and the canaries began to sing.

All at once the captain got up and clapped his hands, and it grew still as could be, all but the merry chuckles of the children. Polly scrambled to the far end of her perch, and hunched herself up as if in a fit of the sulks. Jocko settled down on the captain's shoulder, the little paroquets huddled closely and quietly, and even the canaries twittered about without chirping.

It was growing dark by that time, and the children began putting on their few things, getting ready to go away. It did the kind, generous captain good to see the poor little creatures look so perfectly happy. The tide, which had grown low while the party was aboard, had risen again, and was about as high as when they came, nearly three hours ago. The gang-plank was slanted from the deck as before, and Mr. Hallers and Sam Dickson led each child ashore, and the happiest afternoon in the life of every one of the five was safely ended.

CHAPTER VII.

A CLOUD IN THE SKY.

AFTER the day of the party, Donny continued as before a constant visitor aboard the *Nanetta Masters*. By this time he had become acquainted with the different men making up the officers and crew of the ship, and although Mr. Hallers had become a great favourite because of his hearty welcome, his biscuits, and his nice way of talking to a little lad, yet it was Captain Jack Spliffins that in Donny's eyes and Donny's heart was altogether the kindest, pleasantest, dearest man he had ever known. A few words from him were worth more to the boy than anything else he knew of.

The very sight of the twinkling eyes would send a warm glow of delight all through the little fellow's frame, and he would fly with such genuine joy and affection to meet him, that the captain's own easily touched heart warmed to the little lad, whose quiet, gentlemanly ways always awoke the question as to how he ever happened to hail from a wretched court, and to be of kin to a miserable, ignorant old woman.

But a sea-captain comes across a great many strange, mysterious things in travelling up and down the world, and this was only one of them. And Donny was bright enough to notice some things that a great many children of eight years would never have thought of. With all his jolly ways and merry speeches, the men under Captain Spliffins spoke of him and to him with the greatest respect. And there was something, too, about the captain that made Donny feel sure that, if a man or a boy spoke to him in a manner that they should not, he would in some way make them feel both sorry and ashamed.

He remembered how the birds and monkey obeyed him, yet how lovingly the little monkey kept patting his cheek. "Oh, he's a great, big, kind man, with lots to him," said Donny to himself, and the thought of the manliness of his new friend, and the respect and obedience he demanded and received, was what added to the boy's admiration for him, although he could not have said it in just those words.

"Donald," said the captain one day, as the boy stood watching the sailors using what they called a "holy-stone" in cleaning the deck, "Donald, my boy, what do you expect to do all this long winter, when the weather gets too cold for you to run about the wharf all day?"

"Ho! it's never much too cold for me to run about," said Donny. "I shall be down to Holland Wharf most the time, I guess."

The captain looked sober. "Hum, hum," he said, "I think it is a great pity for a little boy to spend all his time in that way. Why don't you go to school?"

"Granny can't spare me, and, b'sides, I wouldn't like it."

"But can you read or spell?"

"No, sir, guess I don't need to."

"Oh, yes, Donald, every one needs to. You never can make much of a man unless you go to school, and learn to read, write, spell, and to know something of arithmetic and geography. What would I do, or Mr. Hallers, if we had never learned these things? Now I should like to think of my little friend as being in school, and learning all kinds of useful things, after I've gone away. Don't you think you will try and go?"

"I'll ask granny," said Donny, but he spoke so faintly, and looked so troubled, that the captain felt sorry for the child.

The truth was, those dreadful words, "after I've

gone away," smote on Donny's ear as if the whole of his bright little world was about to slip away from him for ever.

"Are — you — goin' very soon?" he asked, as if the words hurt him.

"Not just yet, my boy. but you see we have been in port nearly four weeks. We're going to begin getting in our cargo in a day or two, as soon as a few repairs have been made; then, in the course of about two weeks more, we shall expect to sail away to the other end of the world."

"I wisht I could go to sea when I get to be a man," said Donny, dolefully.

"Then you'll have to study for it, little man," said the captain, sturdily. "You'd better ask your grandmother to let you go to school, and I think perhaps she would. Is she your own grandmother?"

"Yes, I guess so," was the careless reply, "but she won't never let me go to school. Once old Mis' Mellin said she oughter, but granny tole her she couldn't spare me, nor buy the books, and she wouldn't have me gettin' no airs 'bout learnin'. Granny won't let me go to school."

The boy spoke so much as if he was sure of knowing what he was talking about, that the captain was afraid his words were only too true, and as he never could find time to do much on land during the short time between his voyages, he turned away feeling sorry that he could not help this pretty, sweet-tempered little fellow to fit himself properly for the life that was still nearly all before him.

Donny went back to Sunrise Court that night with a heavy pain tugging at his little heart. What should he do when the good ship *Nanetta, Masters* with his dear, dear captain on board, went sailing away to the other end of the world! The thought had not come into his mind before. So happy had he been running off and on the great vessel, talking to the sailors who sometimes tossed him to their backs or shoulders and ran about with him, or joking with Sam Dickson, and crunching down the sweet biscuit that Mr. Hallers was continually crowding into his puny hands, or watching Loo Sing preparing good things of which he always was given a good share. Yes, so happy had he been from day to day, while enjoying all these things, that he had scarcely remembered that the beautiful vessel, so like a lovely home to him, would not always stay in port, and moored at Holland Wharf, and he had never asked what would be the end of it all. Childlike, he had lived, and been very happy just from day to day.

But now, his dear Captain Jack had himself reminded him that it would not be long before the whole delightful "house," as it seemed to the little boy, would sail away out of his sight. Then,—what would Holland Wharf seem like all winter? It was the first great vessel he had ever been on. There never, never would come another like it!

Then, to make matters still worse, a few days afterwards, when they were beginning to get in the cargo, Sam Dickson told Donny that he expected to sail with Captain Spliffins on the next voyage. "And mighty lucky I am to get the chance, too, Mr. Donny."

"Can you read and write?" asked the boy.

"To be sure," answered Sam. "I come under the head of what are called 'able seamen.' I could sail as second mate if the captain needed one, but I'm glad for a berth anyway on the *Nanetta Masters*. I take the place of that sailor that isn't very strong, and wants to take shorter trips. Mostly this vessel takes out pretty much the same crew she brings in. Why, certain, I can read and write; a man ain't fit to do much that's worth anythin', if he doesn't know consid'rable more than jus' readin' and writin'. I've studied navigation; that means all about managin' and steerin' vessels, and usin' charts and compasses, and lots o' things a youngster like you wouldn't know 'bout. A man's got to study to make his way decently in this world."

A few more days had gone by. The *Nanetta Masters* was getting in what was called a "general cargo," such as kerosene oil, pig-iron, quantities of nails, a great quantity of sheetings, and many other things. Donny would sit silent and contented on the deck, where Sam Dickson would "rig up a roost," as he called it, sometimes a mere coil of rope, sometimes a pile of hard canvas, and now and then a stool or backless chair; here the child would never tire of simply looking on, munching biscuit, or eating a delicious orange, or maybe, best of all, talking with a sailor.

He had asked granny about going to school, but she shook her head, said there would be no use of "schoolin'" for the like of him, and that she was afraid it wouldn't be long before he would be a bound-boy. And granny moved about more slowly, and willing Donny helped her more and more, and knew it would not be best to say anything further about going to school. He did not want to go. All that ever made him speak of such a thing was just to please Captain Spliffins.

"But when he gets to the other side of the world he

won't know anything 'bout me," the little boy told himself, sadly, and Sam Dickson said they would be gone a year on the next voyage, and a year is like a life-time to a little fellow of eight.

Still a few more days slipped away. Once in a while the captain would beckon to Donny, and he would know that the great pleasure was before him of going to the cabin, talking to Polly, hearing the paroquets chip and chirp, the cockatoos hop about perking their pretty heads, the canaries sing, and having a frolic with Jocko. Then it almost always happened that Loo Sing would let him go to the kitchen, never failing to treat him to several nice things, and giving him a Chinese napkin full to take home to granny, — poor granny, who took so little notice of her boy now that only once in awhile she washed out his poor little clothes, and tidied up the room. She gave so little attention now to what the boy said, that he told less and less of what he saw at the wharf.

Donny had to look out for Tony Winkers, too, during those days; for the bad, teasing boy had been very angry about being sent away from the ship on the day of the party, although he had only himself to blame for it. More than once Donny crept home to Sunrise Court at night by a roundabout way that made the

WILLING DONNY HELPED HER MORE AND MORE.

trudge much longer for the childish feet; but the fear that Tony might be watching for him made him choose to take more steps, rather than meet the rough, ugly boy. And one night, just before he reached the court, and when he was feeling quite safe, a stone came flying towards him, that sent his little faded cap into the middle of the street.

"Lucky it didn't knock my head off," said Donny, as he picked up the cap, then ran for granny's door.

Then the next morning, as he was twirling along, rushing in all haste for Holland Wharf, Tony came whisking out of a side street, and chased him until he was in sight of the dock, when, coward that he was, Tony shrank back, and left the panting boy to himself.

"Oh, dear!" Donny said, as he came up to Sam Dickson, "I wisht you wasn't goin' away, Sam. There won't be nobody for me to run to, after you're gone, and I'm awful 'fraid o' Tony Winkers, 'cause he's so much bigger'n I be. He's been chasin' me now, so I'm all out o' breath runnin' away from him."

"Why don't you tell a policeman how he torments you?" asked Sam. "Then they'd watch out, and not let him act so like all-possessed."

"But 'twould be dretful for me afterwards, Sam. I ruther never say a word."

Every time Donny thought of Tony that day, he wondered if he would be "layin' for him" when he went home. But there was so much of interest going on, that, after awhile, he forgot everything else but how fast they were getting in the last of the cargo on the great vessel, and it was dark on the short November day when the boy set out for the court, and, although he went home by the usual way, no Tony Winkers was seen or heard from.

CHAPTER VIII.

A CHANGE.

The moment Donny reached Sunrise Court that night, he knew something had happened. Something out of the usual course. There was a brighter light in granny's room than she ever had, and a number of women were standing about the door and in the hall. A horse and buggy stood close to the entrance of the court, and the women were talking so busily they did not see Donny until he was fairly in the hall, looking from one to the other, wondering what the strange feeling that was creeping over him could mean.

"Hist!" said one of the women as she caught sight of him. "Hist! here's the little boy! Oh, now, Donny," she went on, "you won't never see your poor old granny alive any more. She's gone for sure, and none of us here know when she went, either."

Donny's first idea was that his granny had run away.

"But how could she go anywheres, all lame and so

dretful sleepy?" he asked. "And who do you 'xpect went with her?"

"Now, do hear the child!" exclaimed the woman who had spoken before. "It's into a better place she's gone, little boy, and that's where we're all bound for some day, I do hope! But don't you cry nor take on. Mis' Mellin, she says as you can sleep in her room a few nights, then you'll be took care of by some one else. But now run up to Mis' Mellin's room, she's expectin' of you; and be a good boy, then to-morrow you shall look at your granny if you wants to, and p'r'aps you can get your clo'es or anythin' else as b'longs to you."

Donny understood. He remembered how dull and sleepy granny had been getting for weeks, and now he made up his mind that she was growing sick all that time. He knew that people died sometimes, for he had heard granny tell of men and women she used to know, but who were dead now. And then he had never forgotten how a little Timmy Sykes had once been very sick down at Red House Alley, and then had "gone," they said, and he ran with several other children, and looked at the little white, quiet face, and thought, in his oldish way, that it wasn't a very strange thing to die.

Timmy looked better than he had ever seen him look before; and if he was so sound asleep he would never wake up again, that wasn't so very bad, either, because granny said the little boy was still alive in a far better place than Red House Alley, so Donny felt very glad for Timmy, after all.

Now granny had gone to that "better place." Mrs. Parsons had used the same words for it that granny did. But the moment the boy turned to go up the rickety stairs, instead of turning into the old rooms he was used to, it came all over him that granny's going away meant a change for him, and a dreadful feeling of homesickness swept over the child, as he went over the old stairway.

Children and grown people in fine houses have felt the same way, and it makes no difference how poor and miserable the place may be that a child calls "home," it is what he is used to, and what he wants, especially when he does not know what is going to become of him when it fails him.

Donny did not like Mrs. Mellin. "She used to come hobblin' down to granny's room," he thought, "and have lots to say 'bout what she oughter do with me. She used to say I oughter go to school, and I oughtn't to run into the street so much, and I was plenty old 'nuff to go somewheres and earn money."

But Donny had been glad that granny had been one

of the easy kind, and not for ever fussing over him as Mrs. Mellin wanted her to.

"I sha'n't stay with her long," the boy said to himself. Then he stood stock-still outside of Mrs. Mellin's door. "I wonder where will I go, or what they'll do with me," he said.

He felt like running out of the house, but there was Mrs. Parsons and the other women in the entry below, and Mrs. Mellin had heard the boy's slow footsteps on the stairs, and limped across the room. She opened the door rather suddenly, and saw the sober child standing there still as a post.

"There, now, Donny," she began, "you might as well come in, and set right down. There ain't no granny Hilborn left for you to live with, and go errants for, and be made a baby of, any longer. O' course you'll be took care of, somehow, and you must perk up and do jus' as you're tole. You can stay here with me, and have your bed in the corner, and I'll hang up a sheet so's to make a kind o' bedroom for you, and p'r'aps the overseer'll give me granny's money for feedin' of you a little while. And maybe granny left a bit o' money somewheres you may know 'bout. But if they think it's better you should be a bound-boy, seein' you're too small to work 'round here anywheres, why o' course I couldn't do for you long, and you'll have to do jus' as they say. One thing's certain! They won't let you race the streets wild all day no longer, and a good thing it'll be that they won't, too."

"'THEY WON'T LET YOU RACE THE STREETS WILD ALL DAY NO LONGER.'"

Who "they" might be, Donny did not know in the least, but the awful idea of a bound-boy, as pictured by Sam Dickson, arose at once in his troubled mind.

"I couldn't live where there wasn't any water," he

thought; "I know I couldn't; and I wish I could go somewheres and take care o' myself right off."

But Donny did as he was told, and sat quietly down and watched while Mrs. Mellin limped about making some thin porridge for supper. She kept talking in a whining tone, partly to herself and partly to the patient child.

"Now granny's gone," she mumbled, "you won't never know much 'bout what's past and gone, but if she lef' a bit o' money or any writin', you mus' be showin' it to me, 'cause I oughter have some o' her things, seein' as I've know'd her so long."

Donny all at once made up his mind to one thing. Mrs. Mellin was far more concerned about "a bit o' money," or anything of the least value that granny had left and that she could get her hands on, than she was about poor granny's having slipped away, or his future. "She never shall have the old pocketbook," he said to himself, "never; if there's any money in it I'll give it to her, but if granny'd known she was goin' to die, she'd a-given me the old 'purse.'—that's wot she used to call it,—and Mis' Mellin sha'n't even see it, I mean to look out for that."

Way down in that little heart of his, Donny had loved poor old granny, who had done the best she could for him, and he wanted to keep one of the things that had been hers and she had cared for, and with a child's sharp sense he felt sure Mrs. Mellin would say she had been a great friend of granny's, and claim everything she could possibly get.

The next morning Donny was sent for a loaf of bread, and off he started. As he reached granny's door he stopped, wondering if he could get in. He softly turned the loose knob. The door was locked.

"I'm dretful sorry," he said; "I wanted to go in a minute all 'lone by myself."

But after the errand was done, as he went into the entry again, he saw that granny's door was open a little way, and, peeping in, he saw a man standing over by the bed. Something made Donny bold, for he stepped inside the room, and as the man turned around he said:

"I used to live here; that's my granny over there, and I — I — wants to get somethin'."

The boy's face was of a kind to make any one believe in him, and the man said, not unkindly:

"All right, little feller, if there's anything you want, now's your time; go ahead and get it. I'll have to lock up when I go out."

Donny went to the little cupboard, took down the heavy old sugar-bowl, and in a moment the worn pocketbook was hidden in his jacket. But first he had looked into it, and took out the sum of seventeen cents. This he put into another pocket.

"Have you seen your grandmother?" asked the man, as the child turned to go out.

"No, sir."

"Well, don't you want to?"

Donny went at once to the side of the bed. Granny looked exactly as if she was asleep, — just as she used to look before getting up in the morning.

"Now, if I were you," said the man, "I'd kiss grandmother, and then not look at her again. They'll have a prayer here this afternoon, and perhaps a bit of Bible reading, but you'd better always remember grandmother lying asleep in bed, all natural and comfortable. That's my *advice*." And the man smiled down at the child.

"Yes, I'll do that," said Donny, in his mild, gentlemanly little way.

He kissed the withered old cheek, the stranger lifting him to the tall bed, touched granny's hand lightly, gave a long, long look at the peaceful face, said "good-bye" to the man who had treated him so kindly, and turned away. So he always remembered granny sleeping quietly in her own bed.

"Now what kep' you so long?" complained Mrs. Mellin, as he went to her room with the bread. Donny replied at once:

"There was a nice man in granny's room, and he said I better see her. I did, and I ain't a-goin' to look at her again. Here's some money I found where she always kep' it. I brought it for you to have;" and the boy handed over the seventeen cents.

"Where did your granny keep her money?" asked the old woman, sharply, as she grabbed what Donny held out to her.

"She always kep' it in an ole sugar-bowl, and I brought you all there was."

As Donny had been told there would be, there was a prayer, and reading from the Bible, that afternoon, in granny's room. Mrs. Mellin, Mrs. Parsons, and all the women of the court, with two or three men, were gathered in the little room and entry. Donny sat on the stairs, heard the prayer and the reading, then went back to Mrs. Mellin's room.

Mrs. Parsons found him there, and asked if he didn't want to see his granny once more, but he said "No," in a way that made her think it would be of no use to urge him, so she went away. Then, after a little while, Mrs. Mellin came sighing and grunting over the stairs, there was a sound of wheels outside, and the old court settled down to its usual quiet.

Donny had been in the dreary old house all day, and was thinking how perfectly beautiful it would be to get back to the lovely great vessel the next morning, when Mrs. Mellin said, crossly:

"I ain't a-goin' to have you runnin' no one knows where, all the time whilst I take care o' you, and to-morrow they're goin' to make up their minds wot to do with you. I saw the overseer jus' now, and they won't give no extra money on your 'count. The city is goin' to look out for you right away, so you might's well get ready for a change."

That night Donny could not go to sleep. He lay very still, thinking of that coming "change," and was thankful Mrs. Mellin had not said, "You shall not go out of the house to-morrow." He would at any rate have one more blessed day on the *Nanetta Masters*. It must be very near time for her to sail. Then what should he do?

So forlorn was the child that something came back into his mind that he had heard that afternoon, and noticed. The man who prayed in granny's room said,

"And, O God, take care of the little boy that now is left alone."

"I wonder if the great God will care for a speck of a boy like me," Donny thought, and while he was wondering about it, he fell asleep.

CHAPTER IX.

BETWEEN DECKS.

AFTER Donny got the stale loaf in the morning, he slipped it into the room while Mrs. Mellin's back was turned, then ran nimbly away. He was soon aboard the beloved vessel, and knew by all he saw that the last preparations were being made for sailing.

"We start to-morrow, at high tide," said Sam Dickson, looking the other way as he spoke. "It will be pretty nigh on to dusk, and most dark."

Never were the men kinder to the child than to-day. They knew what had happened, but understood that some other old woman was to take charge of the little boy, and, although they said nothing to him about his loss, his hands were full of the fruits and cakes they showered upon him.

The captain found time to say a few kind words, and gave him a shining quarter, but he was called away before he had said half the things that were in his heart.

Donny heard from Mr. Hallers that the vessel would sail, rain or shine; that the men were to be aboard by noon the next day. "And you might come for a call at noon, yourself, little mate," he added, in an off-hand way.

At night Mrs. Mellin was snappish and sour, and scolded Donny, roundly, for running off and staying all day, but she grew a little milder at sight of the nice fruits the boy had brought with him, though she still went on with her fault-finding.

"Oh, come now, Mis' Mellin," said the more kindly Mrs. Parsons, who happened to be in the room, "why don't you let the boy have a little peace when it's only to-morrow he'll be round, anyway? His granny let him go as he wanted to, and a good boy he was to her, too. I've heard granny Hilborn say so many's the time; now, I'd favour him a bit before he goes away, I would that!"

Donny felt sure it would be of no use to ask Mrs. Mellin any questions, but the next day, as he was coming back from an errand, he met Tom Smart, and he asked Donny where he was going. "I don't know," he replied; "do you?"

"No," said Tom, "but my marm says as how a man was to see Mis' Mellin yes'day, and it's all fixed up that you're to be took off somewheres to-morrow mornin'."

Donny swallowed hard, but made no reply. His life of freedom was all ended, and he might as well make up his mind to it. He stayed at the court through the morning, helping Mrs. Mellin all he could, but nothing suited her. At noon he was thankful to slip off, in the direction of the wharf.

"My last time," he said, with a mournful little face that would have made any mother's heart ache. "Captain Jack's goin' away, and I'm goin' away, and there won't be a Holland Wharf to see any more, nor I sha'n't be Donny any more."

Poor child! He felt as if he really would be some other boy without granny, without Captain Jack, without the vessel, and without the wharf, his playground and his delight.

"I may die," he murmured. "Timmy Sykes died, and so did granny. P'r'aps I'll die pretty soon." It seemed to be all the relief of which the child could think.

At the wharf there appeared to be no chance to speak to anybody. Donny ran to the deck with two sailors who were just going aboard. After an hour Mr. Hallers passed near him, and with a smart little rap on his back said, cheerfully:

"Well, we sea-birds are about flying, little mate; keep up good heart, we'll be back some day."

"Could I go to the cabin just once more?" asked Donny.

"I'm afraid not," said the mate. "I wish you could, but captain's having a few last words with a man that's sending out some drillings, and it might disturb him. You might stay a little while longer, but the tide's rising, and, if I were you, I guess I wouldn't stay aboard till the last minute; it'll only make you feel worse. Wait a minute."

He disappeared, then soon came in sight again with a little tin box full of the crisp biscuit Donny liked as much as many of the cakes Loo Sing made. "There! God bless you, little mate; keep a good stiff upper lip, and we'll be back one o' these days."

He put the box in Donny's hands, then turned without saying good-bye, and hurried away as if he thought of something, and might return. It was his way of leaving the child without saying he was leaving him.

Donny went over to where Sam Dickson was talking with the pilot of the steam-tug that was to tow them out into the stream. For a little while he roamed about, then the captain came on deck, and, seeing the boy, spoke very kindly to him.

"P'r'aps I'll go to school," was all Donny could think of to say.

"That's right, I hope you will, little man," said the captain; "and you must watch out when Captain Jack Spliffins will come sailing into port again, and be on hand to say 'how-dy-do.' Some one wants me, and I may be back in a few moments."

Then Sam Dickson found time to talk with him a little while, and when he was suddenly called to attend to some duty Donny remembered what the mate had kindly said to him about not staying until he had to go at the last moment, so he tried to speak bravely, and, although his voice sounded strange and far-off to himself, he said, with a poor, piteous little smile:

"Good-bye, Sam, I guess I'll go now, and I sha'n't watch the vessel sail off."

"Well, now, that's uncommon wise for a peep o' your years," said Sam, brightly, "and good day, little feller; I won't forget the little comrade that got me a job, but be a man, and good luck to you!" and Sam waved his hand cheerily as the boy at once left the deck.

Donny went part way down the slant gang-plank,

watched the men several minutes on the steam-tug, then turned for a last look at the beloved *Nanetta Masters*. His poor little heart was bursting. He thought of the happy, happy hours he had spent on board, by far the happiest of his life. He thought how in two or three hours the great, home-like vessel would go sailing over the water, her lights flashing, the captain in his cosy cabin with the pets about him; thought of Loo Sing in the cook-room, preparing nice dishes for the captain and the mate, of the warm-hearted sailors going to and fro, and then — of himself, in Mrs. Mellin's dingy room, waiting to be taken away to-morrow from even a sight of Holland Wharf!

"Oh, I can't! I can't!" cried the little, sobbing child. "I ruther die! I'd ruther they'd throw me overboard! I'd ruther — anythin'!"

He gave a wild look around. Something was drawing the attention of the men to the far end of the deck. The men on the steam-tug were all busy, having no eyes for a little, broken-hearted boy who could scarcely see through the tears as he peered anxiously at them for an instant.

Quick as a flash back darted the lad. The sailors on deck were tugging at a great coil of rope, their backs turned towards him. One of the hatchways was open;

down rushed the boy "between decks," where a part of the cargo was closely piled, and in a moment there was a little stowaway — although he did not know that was what he would be called — on the brave ship *Nanetta Masters*, bound for the China seas.

But a dreadful trial was coming.

A pair of sharp, evil eyes had seen the scrambling legs that went rushing back to the vessel's deck.

"Hoorah! I wonder if little old Donny Hilborn thinks two can't play at that game!" cried Tony Winkers, under his breath. "Wonder if he thinks I don't know he means to hook passage on the big ship that's bound for Chiny!" And the boy ran swiftly for the gang-plank.

Although Tony had a better home than ever Donny had with granny Hilborn, yet he was always in trouble with his parents because of his bad temper and naughty tricks; so no sooner did he see poor Donny glance quickly about, then run for the deck, than he knew what it meant. He thought what one boy could do, another could.

"Ho, Mister Donny!" he went on, "I've been wantin' and threat'nin' to run away for a good while, and they say the cap'n's that good that he couldn't hurt a flea; so if you're takin' a trip to Chiny, I'll go too; might's well have two boys aboard as only one."

So fast and so soon did Tony follow Donny, that the sailors had not looked around when he reached the deck and scaled the rail, and he was just in time to see the top of Donny's fair little head disappearing down the hatchway; but when he landed between decks, the first boy had already got out of sight.

"Donny! Donny!" he called, softly. "I know you! I'm here, too!" And although Donny had hidden himself so completely that Tony could not see or find him, he heard the bad boy tucking himself away, almost close by him, and he knew the tormenting Tony Winkers was going to be his fellow passenger.

For a few moments Donny thought he must come right out, tell the captain what he meant to do, and that Tony Winkers was on board, then beg the kind captain, with all his might and main, to take him on the voyage.

But, no; Mr. Hallers had told how once a gentleman wanted the captain to take his little son on a voyage, and the captain had stoutly refused, saying he couldn't have the care of a little shaver on shipboard, he seldom took passengers, never children.

But for all that, Donny had almost made up his

mind to tell the captain, even if he was sent ashore, when he thought of a "bound-boy," and the dreadful words kept him quiet. Anything but that!

After a long, long time, to the worried boy, there was a sound of feet running to and fro, a straining of ropes, calls here and there, a hissing and puffing from the tug, and slowly at first, quite slowly, the *Nanetta Masters* slipped away from her anchorage at Holland Wharf; some friends on shore cried out a few jovial words of parting, and the long journey was begun.

There was still a good deal of running to and fro for another hour, then it was growing quieter, when something happened that set Donny trembling in every joint.

It began quietly enough. Just a little clanking sound, as of some one dragging a small chain over a part of the ship near where he lay hidden. Then, only a few steps from his hiding-place, arose a fretful, scolding, angry chattering. It increased, growing louder and louder, until a sailor came running up, exclaiming:

"Aha! here is the little wretch! Come here, Jocko! Don't you know better than to run away, and go clattering off 'tween decks, when cap'n's good enough to give you the length o' the cabin to go a-trampoosin' about in? Grandfather! who have we here?" — Oh, how the sailor's voice had altered! — "Come out o' that, *you boy!* Goin' to hook passage to Chiny, was you! Well, we'll spoil that fun for you, quick shot!"

The angry sailor seemed to be pulling Tony out of his cubby, as he called out:

"Cap'n! Cap'n! p'r'aps you'd like to see a piece o' cargo that Jocko, here, helped me find; will you please look here, sir?"

Donny could not hear the captain's step as plainly as he had heard the chain of the little runaway monkey, but he did hear Captain Jack Spliffins's voice, as he lumbered to the spot just beyond him, and, oh, dear! *could* it be his Cap'n Jack who was speaking in a tone like that?

"It strikes me you're the same boy that used to make trouble for smaller lads on land," said the captain, in his terrible voice. "So you thought it would be a fine thing to take a sea voyage, did you? Well, I'd serve you right, sir, to tie you to the yard-arm, and give you a few good cuts, such as you'd always remember!" Tony tried to speak.

"No answering!" said the captain, raising his voice.

"'Tisn't the fashion, on shipboard, to answer the captain. A boy that tries to steal a passage aboard ship is a coward, sir, and what you want to get out of your nature is the coward there is in it!"

"Oh, but please, sir,—" began Tony again. Donny knew he was doing his best to tell about him.

"Silence!" thundered the captain, "not a word out of your mouth! I want no excuses! You have none to offer. Now you will come with me and stay by yourself, where I put you, for about an hour. It's foggy, and we are to be towed well out; then you'll be put aboard the tug, and sent ashore where you belong. You will not be treated unkindly, but not a word are you to speak to any one, from this moment until land is reached again. If you disobey, I shall give the pilot strict orders to have you well punished for trying to steal a passage on my vessel."

Donny was afraid that, in the face of the captain's severe threat, Tony would blurt out, "There's another boy aboard." That would be enough to send him back, also, but he remembered what a coward Tony really was, and hoped that the fear of certain punishment, if he disobeyed, would keep him quiet. He thought he should know when the tug loosened from the great vessel, and started back with Tony on board. But

BONNY AS A STOWAWAY.

the little boy was very, very tired; he had not slept until quite late the night before, from sheer heartache, so as matters quieted he ate a few of the biscuits in the tin box, then fell into a deep, sweet sleep.

CHAPTER X.

DOWN THE ATLANTIC OCEAN.

When Donny awoke it was broad daylight, and he knew that to be so bright at that season of the year it could not be very early in the morning.

On first waking, all he could think of was how cramped he felt, for he was wedged in between great bales, the rows packed so closely that it had been only in a narrow passage between several rows that he had found a little place where he could sit on one bale, with his back against another.

After stretching a little, he felt more at ease. Then the next feeling that crept over him was one of perfect thankfulness that he was on the beautiful, great ship, as it had always been to him, ever since the first day he ever went on deck, and that she was getting well out to sea.

No matter what else happened, they could not send him back now. Tony Winkers was home in New York, and a new feeling of joy swept over Donny as he thought, no matter how many tales Tony told now, "they," the dreaded men who were going to send him away, could not stretch out a long arm, and pull him off from the *Nanetta Masters*. Yet in his heart Donny resolved not to let any one know he was on board until his biscuits gave out.

"If I'm careful," he whispered, "I can make them last all day to-day, and all day to-morrow, — and how beautiful it is to be here!"

That was all the poor little fellow could think of. Staying all by himself, counting bales, and watching the shadows come and go, did not tire him as it would have tired most boys. Once in awhile there would be a rolling motion to the vessel that amused him greatly. He slept now and then without knowing it, and, sheltered as he was, he did not feel cold, — not very.

Towards night, the sea grew rough, there was the sound of rain, the wind whistled, almost screamed, and Donny could hear the sailors tramping about; sometimes coming so near he shrank up into a mere knot of a boy, that never could have been seen in the darkness unless a lantern had been flashed directly over him. Yet he was glad he was there.

The night passed, and on the day that followed the biscuits were gone entirely. It was late on still the next day, the third one out, that a very hungry and a very much frightened little fellow knew he must go to the captain, confess what he had done, and throw himself on the captain's mercy. He remembered how Tony had been dealt with, remembered that dear Captain Jack had called him a coward, and now —

"But I won't stop to think about it any longer," said Donny, trying to feel as brave as he could. "I'll jus' go tell cap'n the truth, then he can throw me overboard if he's angry 'nuff; that would be better'n bein' a bound-boy."

Captain Spliffins was seated in his armchair at the cabin table, bending over the "log-book," in which is kept the ship's records, busily writing. A large lamp was swinging slightly in a snug frame above his head, and, as he kept at work, Polly suddenly screamed, "Oh, my! Who are you? Who are you? Come in, take a seat! Take a seat! Oh, what a fright! Ha! ha! ha!"

As Polly ceased, a little sound near the entrance of the cabin caused Captain Spliffins to turn his head. For a moment it seemed as though he saw a spirit. There stood a little boy, so white and scared that his little face looked almost all eyes, with a mass of fair hair a little above them. There was that about the poor, pitiful little object that kept the captain perfectly quiet. The next moment the small figure crept up to his chair, and, partly from fear, partly from weakness,

"THERE STOOD A LITTLE BOY, SO WHITE AND SCARED."

sat down on the floor, folded his hands, and said, in a thin, piping little voice:

"Oh, please, cap'n, please! They were goin' to send me away. I was goin' to be a bound-boy, and I ruther 'a' died! I'd ruther you, or Mr. Hallers, or Sam Dickson'd throw me overboard; but I'll be a dretful good boy if you'll let me work at somethin' — "

Just then Polly helped poor Donny, for she croaked in her queer, cramped voice, " Oh, my, what a fool! What a fool! Tie him up! Tie him up! Oh, my! Oh, my!"

As the captain turned, and looked at the saucy bird, Donny noticed how sober his face was. He thought what a *dear* face it was, too, and how he loved it; but when the captain slowly turned back, looked down at him, and, without a word, shook his head, sadly, sorrowfully, the child started up, with all his hungry little heart aching for love from somebody, and, running to the back of the chair, flung his arms around the captain's neck, and, with his face flat against the broad back, he cried and sobbed until his little body shook about like a frail leaf blown by the wind.

Donny was not very clean; he had been a poor, neglected child, and Captain Jack Spliffins, with all his easy ways and loosely fitting garments, was extremely neat and nice in all his habits. Now, he took hold of Donny's thin little arm, drew him towards him, turned in the revolving chair, and, seating the boy on his knees, took hold of both his arms, holding him tight without exactly hugging him up.

"Little man," he said, in a low voice, "do you think it was right to come on board my vessel without asking leave?"

"N-o," sobbed Donny, "but you wouldn't 'a' took me. I wouldn't ever 'a' come if granny hadn't 'a' died. I'd never 'a' run away from granny. I always 'bey'd her when she was 'live. But Mis' Mellin warn't nice. She didn't love me, nor want me, and a man come to the court, and was goin' to take me 'way where I wouldn't 'a' had no wharf, nor the *Nanetta Masters* any more, nor nothin'. I didn't mean to be bad, nor a coward, but I — I — was mos' dead, and I come aboard 'cause I couldn't help it."

"Did that Winkers boy come with you?"

"No, no! he must 'a' seen me, and followed jus' to plague me. B'sides, he wanted to run away from his folks. I wouldn't 'a' come with him for anythin'; he's a dretful bad boy, Tony is. But I couldn't be a bound-boy! I ruther die."

"Very well. Now I sha'n't scold you, Donald, nor say anything to make you more unhappy. You did wrong, but it is some different with a lad who has no parents to try finding a home for himself, from what it is for a wilful boy to run away. But I am master here, and you will have to do exactly as I say. Seeing you have put yourself in my care, I shall try to teach you; there will be lessons to learn every day, and you shall study right here in the cabin. There will be some work for you to do, too. At other times, you will be allowed to go about the vessel and amuse yourself as long as you are obedient, and do not make any trouble. When did you have anything to eat, boy?"

"I had some biscuit Mr. Hallers give me, but they was all gone las' night."

"Sit down there," and the captain pointed to the soft lounge; "I have matters to attend to, and must leave you alone for the present."

"Please, please, will you forgive me?" The boy's voice was weak, and full of tears.

The pressure of the fair little head was still felt along the captain's back, and, looking at the young face full of eagerness for his forgiveness, he said, still soberly:

"Yes, Donald, I'll forgive you, and if you obey me and study well, I will have you for one of my little friends."

Donny choked as the big captain rolled away. But

joy is much nearer the heart of a child than sorrow, and for all he still felt sorry that he had done wrong, yet the boy's heart was already beginning to sing within him, and he could not push down the happy feeling that was spreading all through his little soul and body.

He was aboard the *Nanetta Masters;* Tony Winkers was even now many miles away. "They" would not find him when "they" went to Sunrise Court to carry him away. No fear of being a bound-boy now. And, oh, joy! he was going to be his dear captain's little friend. No question as to being obedient found a place in the boy's happy mind.

In about ten minutes Loo Sing stood at the entrance of the cabin, smiling and beckoning. How delightful to see the generous cook again! But Donny did not stir.

"Captain told me to stay here, Loo."

"Cappee say, 'go gettee boy.' Gettee dinner. Cappee say have dinner."

At that Donny went willingly enough. The Chinaman led the way to the pantry, pointed to a high stool beside a wide form, and said:

"Sittee, sittee, eatee, eatee, all velly hungree, eatee lot."

A plate filled with food, and a mug of weak coffee, smelling grandly, were welcome sights to Donny. He climbed to the seat, and ate all he could, which was a little more than half that Loo Sing had set forth, but the coffee tasted most delightfully of all.

He had just jumped to the floor when the vessel gave a queer lurch, and he banged against the side of the wall. Loo looked around with a wide, serene smile.

"No catchee wallee in big storm," he said. "All go rolly, rolly, tumblee, tumblee long a floor."

Donny giggled merrily, and went back to the cabin. The captain was there, and said he wanted to talk to him a little while. "I shall teach you to read, write, and spell," he said, "and Mr. Hallers will show you how to take care of the pets. It will be your work each day."

"Oh, I'm glad! I shall like that;" and Donny smiled at the thought.

"It won't be play, my boy; neither can it be done in a moment. It will take time and care, and yet it will not be hard work, nor take too much strength. When you begin you must go right on, not stopping to play, or leaving off for anything else. Jocko is sponged, combed, and brushed every day. If he scratches you,

I shall switch him, and he will behave himself. Poll will make all kinds of remarks, but do not stop to talk with her or teach her new words while cleaning the cage. If she claws or snaps at you, as she may do at first, she will be kept in the dark for an hour or two, and will soon understand she is to make no trouble. The other birds are always gentle, and would be timid, only they have been so kindly treated they are very tame. You will never harm them, I know. You are to sleep in the stateroom with Hallers, the first mate. There is an alcove to it that can be partly shut off, where we can fix up a comfortable berth."

In a week's time Donny felt like a new boy. He really was a new boy, leading a new life. He was learning to be neat, useful, and studious. Mr. Tom Hallers was secretly delighted that the boy was aboard; so was Sam Dickson, Loo Sing, and every sailor aboard the ship. Yet no one said so to Donny; it might not have been best.

Donny learned something every day. As they passed the Bermudas, Mr. Hallers, who never tired of his questions, told the little fellow of the beautiful soft airs of the islands belonging to Great Britain, and of the fine vegetables that vessels carried from them to the markets at New York and Boston.

One night, when they had been some weeks on the voyage, it became very hard for Donny to keep on his feet. How the sailors managed he could not understand, but they appeared to pitch with the vessel, and keep their footing. The wind rushed and whirled about the great floating house, and when he tried to go "for'ard" to the deck-house, where Sam Dickson had a bunk with the other sailors, he tripped, and rolled along the boards.

"Steady, there, little mate," said a sailor who picked him up, and was himself on the way to the fo'c's'l. "Better come alongside, and let me tow you. We're in for a night of it. The sea is black as Egypt, and there won't be much rest for some o' us on the *Nanetta*, I'm thinkin', 'cordin' to the way we're pitchin' it now."

All the evening the wind and storm increased. Sam Dickson helped Donny back to the cabin, where he could hear at times the captain's voice, sounding like a mighty roar, as he gave commands through the ship's trumpet. There was hard, steady effort on the part of the crew to keep the stanch vessel to her course, and not once did Donny feel in the least afraid. In fact, he got considerable fun out of it all. Mr. Hallers had told him not to leave the cabin again.

"Sit right on the lounge," said the mate, as Donny tried to seat himself in a corner. The next moment he rolled to the floor.

"Can't stay," said the laughing boy, as he clutched at a leg of the table.

"I'll have to strap you on," said Mr. Hallers.

"Oh, no, let me roll," said Donny, who enjoyed the scramble to and fro.

"No, sir! You'd be black and blue before morning, and stiff as an old man of a hundred." And seizing a strap with a stout buckle to it, Hallers soon had the lad fastened to the lounge in such a way that he could either sit up or lie down without danger of rolling off.

Two hours afterwards, somewhere past midnight, the captain came staggering to the cabin, to Donny's amusement; but he kept on his feet, reached his armchair, then, opening a drawer side of the table, took out a strap, and fastened himself to the chair.

"Great doings, isn't it, my boy?" he asked, his eyes twinkling as if he, too, saw the funny side of it all. "Well, this is rather a mild storm at sea."

"Mild?" cried Donny, opening his eyes in surprise.

"Oh, yes, this doesn't amount to much, and the worst of it is over. I've told Loo to bring me some tea, and you may possibly see a circus before I get it.

I'm a little tired, and shall try to get a nap in my chair. You may turn in if you want to."

But Donny didn't want to "turn in." He was excited, and wide awake, and liked his safe resting-place on the lounge.

In a few minutes, Loo Sing came slipping softly into the cabin with a cup of tea on a tray. He was but a few steps from the captain, when — crack!

Down went Loo, tray, cup of tea, and all, a steaming mass on the cabin floor.

"Oh, what a fool!" screamed Polly. "Ha! ha! ha! My, what a fool!" Then she croaked, dismally, "Land! What a row! What a row! Here we go down — down — down!"

Donny laughed until he nearly choked. Loo got upon his feet, gathered up his tray, and the thick cup, which had not broken, and, smiling sweetly, was slipping back to the pantry, when Polly screamed after him, "Come back! Come back!" And as the calm Chinaman looked over his shoulder, the sly bird croaked, "Pick up the tea! Pick up the tea!"

Donny fairly rolled about under his strap, and the captain's broad shoulders gave a shudder of laughter at the boy's amusement.

Loo came back in a very short time, went nimbly

across the cabin, tray in hand, and the captain had his hand out to take the tea, when there came a tremendous lurch, and back went the Chinaman, his pigtail flying out straight from his head as he slapped one hand, hard, on the table in trying to save himself. The cup actually bounced along the floor, and the tray landed on the lounge, while Loo's heels flew up in the air as he went backwards with a crack that seemed as if it might have snapped his spine.

"Oh! oh! oh!" screeched Poll. "Here we go down — down — down!"

Donny nearly lost his breath in the gasps of laughter he tried to stop for poor Loo's sake, while Polly kept up a groaning of "Oh, sad! sad! sad!"

To the boy's relief, Loo picked himself up again, smiling as ever, took up the tray, found the cup, still unbroken, and started out again on his errand.

"Bring a mug in your hand, without any tray, the next time, Loo," advised the captain. "Oh, what a fool!" muttered Polly, as the man went up the companionway.

The patient cook came a third time, with only a mug. Little slops of tea fell over the towel he had been thoughtful enough to wind around his hand; and this time he reached the captain without falling. Polly again complimented him on being a fool, but his placid face beamed on Donny as smilingly as ever as he asked, "Have a cup o' tea?"

"No, I do not want any tea, thank you, Loo," said the lad, politely.

In a few moments more, both the tired captain and the little mate were fast asleep.

CHAPTER XI.

LAND, HO!

Donny was talking with Loo Sing, one morning, in the cook-room, when there was a cry of "Land, ho!" from the sky, as it seemed. The boy ran to the deck, and saw one of the sailors way up in the rigging of the foremast, who kept singing out, "Land, ho!"

Captain Jack was soon on deck, spy-glass in hand. "Yes," he said, "we shall make St. Helena before sun-down. That lonely island, lying in the ocean on our way around the cape, was once a volcano, my boy. Now, you don't know what that means. But on that island we have sighted, is a very high hill, pointed at the top. What should you think to see a great cloud of fire and smoke going way up, till it appeared to touch the sky, from that hilltop, and sending ashes, stones, and bits of rock far out to sea?"

"Shall we see that?"

"No, Donald, because the volcano is dead. 'Extinct,' we call it. It has ceased to burst into flame and smoke. But, if we should land, you would see strange rows of what is called 'lava,' white ashes, and stone, that form regular rows around the hill.

"Once there was a man so fond of power and conquest — that is, of getting the victory in battle — that he became a great general, and was as fond of war as a boy like you is of sport. He won victory after victory, not that he might do good, and help the people who came under his rule, but just to have the right to govern, and make of himself the greatest man in the world. He wanted to win the world, if he could, through war and bloodshed. But after he and his troops lost the great battle of Waterloo, in Belgium, — you must study all about these things some day, little man, — he was sent to the island of St. Helena, this lonely rock in mid-ocean, to live by himself the rest of his life.

"Think of it! For nearly six long years he was there under the guard of English soldiers. He had got away once after being sent to the island of Elba, in the Mediterranean Sea, but this time the English nation did not mean that he should escape again to stir up war and confusion."

"Tell me more about him, please."

"There is but little more that you would understand. But one of these days, when you study history, and learn all about Napoleon Bonaparte, he will look to you like a very great man. And he was a very great man indeed; but remember, he was also a very dangerous man, because, with all his knowledge of other men, and skill in warfare, he was selfish and cruel, and cared more for his own fame and great name than for the lives of thousands of his fellow men."

Then the captain went away, and Donny ran for the cabin, as it was time to see to the pets, then to study. He could already read a little, and was learning to write and to spell easy words. He liked his lessons, which were regular, and when it was not convenient for the captain to attend to them, Mr. Hallers enjoyed teaching the willing little pupil.

When the vessel passed the island of St. Helena, all hands were on deck, and Mr. Hallers told Donny a few stories of the great Napoleon.

"I'd like to be a great man some day," said Donny, with shining eyes.

Just then Mr. Hallers exclaimed, "Oh, look, boy! see! there's the head of a shark, — over there, to the right!"

Donny looked, and saw the large head and dreadful open mouth of an enormous creature that was following the vessel at a little distance.

"That fellow hopes to get some food out of us," said the mate; while Donny looked in surprise at the rows and rows of sharp, awful teeth.

"I suppose he'd eat me, bones and all, if he could get me," said Donny, with his amused little grin.

"Sakes!" exclaimed Mr. Hallers, "there's nothing, on the broad earth or in the deep sea that Mr. Shark likes any better than 'little boy pie.' He enjoys 'man pudding' pretty well, but wouldn't he smack those great jaws of his if he could only get hold of a tender morsel like the little mate of the *Nanetta Masters*, Donny Hilborn by name!"

Donny was going through a series of little chuckles when Mr. Hallers turned to him suddenly, a new idea in his mind.

"See here, little mister, didn't you say Jocko had been behaving very bad of late, whenever you try to clean and comb him?"

"Yes, he acts awfully. I don't like to tell on him, but I had to run all over the cabin, and catch him three or four times this mornin', while I was cleanin' him."

"Well, I don't approve of frightening any kind of an animal just for the fun of it," began Mr. Hallers, "but it'll just surprise you to see how we'll break up Mr. Jock's antics at bathing-time, by treating him to a look at Mr. Shark. You go down to the cabin, and begin combing him; then, when he gets pretty highty-tighty, I'll waltz in, catch him up, and show him that fellow swimming alongside. You won't have any more trouble with that small rebel before we land."

Donny went to the cabin, comb in hand, at sight of which Jocko uttered an angry cry, then chattered and scolded, monkey-fashion, with all his might. Whether the little fellow felt it was too bad to be cleaned twice a day, or whether he was making up his little monkey mind not to let Donny look after his monkeyship any longer, no one could say, but he really showed his teeth, and, running out a paw, scratched Donny sharply when he tried to rub him down.

At that Mr. Hallers made his appearance. "Now you shall see a few teeth, too," he said, and, taking Jocko in his arms, he twined the chain about his arm with Donny's help, while Jocko winked and blinked solemnly, first at one, then the other, as if he wondered what the performance meant.

When the deck was reached, Mr. Hallers went to the gunwale, holding Jocko firmly by the shoulders, and allowing him to view the water. All at once the shark raised its thick head and body half-way out of the water.

Jocko gave a piercing cry, then another, and another, trying with all his strength to shrink back against the mate; but Hallers held him where his terrified eyes were fixed on the monster, now quite close to the vessel's side. But the fright and trembling of the little animal were so painful that after a moment the mate let go his strong hold, when Jocko scrambled inside his heavy jacket and out of sight in an instant.

"Now I'm going to make him understand it's you he's got to mind," said Hallers, and, drawing on the chain, he made the little sobbing creature come out into daylight, and handed him over to Donny.

The boy's gentle hand went over the soft coat of the shaking monkey with a soothing touch, but it made him laugh to see the whites of Jocko's eyes rolling up at him in a droll, beseeching way, as he clung to the boy as if for dear life, keeping his face against his arm, and as far away from the dreaded gunwale as he could get it. With a feeling of real pity for the dumb pet, Donny said:

"I guess he understands now, Mr. Hallers; may I take him below?"

"Oh, certainly; he's all cured by this time, and he's the most perfect gentleman aboard the *Nanetta Masters* for the rest of this voyage, you see if he isn't!"

And sure enough. On being placed in his corner, little Jocko turned his face to the wall, and shrank into such a ball of disconsolate fur that Polly called out in a voice of scorn, "Oh, my! What a fright! What a fright! Put 'im out! Put 'im out!"

The next morning, Jocko, all of himself, held out first one paw, then another, to be sponged and rubbed, putting his cute little head to one side with a coaxing look from his bright eyes that set Donny into fits of laughter, when afterwards he told Mr. Hallers of the monkey's beautiful behaviour. And for more than a week no one could coax the poor little thing up the companionway, even by the offer of lumps of sugar.

"He's cured, sure!" said Mr. Hallers, as at sight of the mate the monkey would scramble under the lounge.

When they were rounding the Cape of Good Hope, the captain said, "If we were in distress, Donald boy, here is where we should put in, at Cape Town, way down at the southern point of Africa. It would amuse you to see the ostriches, with their beautiful feathers flaunting behind them, scudding along on their long, slender legs. They are queer birds. When frightened, they run and poke their heads in the sand, and think because they cannot see anything that they are all out of sight, and safe. I think their eggs are the largest ones there are; they often weigh three pounds each. Beautiful stones, called diamonds, are found there, too."

There came a night soon after this, when the *Nanetta Masters* strained every timber, it appeared to Donny, in trying to keep herself together. At last the storm became so violent that Donny was alone in the cabin for hours, strapped, as once before, to the lounge. When a sailor ran to the cabin on a hasty errand, the boy asked if there was any danger.

"Well, it's 'bout as dangerous as I should care to see it," was the reply. Then Polly took up the cheerful cry, "Oh, sad! sad! Here we go, down — down — down!"

Donny laughed a little, then grew thoughtful. For the first time since going aboard he thought of the minister's prayer in granny's room, and the little boy showed more faith than many men sometimes do, for he said, fearlessly, "God has taken care of me, splendid care! He let me get on to the ship I loved, and I'm all safe long as he looks out for me."

All the next day the wild storm raged. Loo Sing carried food to the cabin in strong dishes for Donny, but the captain and mate took hurriedly what they wanted in the pantry. Donny was not allowed to leave the cabin, although he longed to get across to the

JOCKO REFORMS.

fo'c's'l, and hear what the sailors had to say. At night the wind went down, but the sea was still very rough, and the vessel plunged heavily. The captain, well worn out, reached his armchair, but did not attempt to sleep.

"Frightened, little mate?" he asked, the old twinkle in his eyes.

"No, sir."

"Why not? This has been a tough one, and no mistake."

Donny's face flushed a bit, but he answered at once, "A man at granny's asked God to take care of me, and he has, and — he will."

"That's right, Donald, that's right." Then the captain asked, suddenly, "Didn't your grandmother ever tell you anything at all about your father or your mother? Or didn't you ever hear her speak of them in any way?"

The boy's eyes opened wide in innocent surprise: "No, sir; granny never told me much about anything," he said.

"I hope you'll make a good man one of these days," the captain added, but he spoke wearily, and more as if talking to himself than to any one else.

"I haven't got any folks lef' to take care o' me," the boy said, simply.

"That may be very true, little man," and the captain seemed to wake up, and speak more brightly, "but I know a man — he lives in China, too, and is a great friend of mine — who, when a boy, had a rich father, with a proud old name; but while he was still quite young my friend's mother died, then the father lost his money, and soon died, too, leaving his son without a relation in the world. But while he was still a mere lad, he made up his mind that any money he was ever likely to have he had got to make for himself, and that if he ever was to become much of a man, that must be his own lookout, also. To-day, he has one of the most beautiful homes I know of. Some day I will take you to see it."

Then the captain was called away, and Donny sat dreaming of what he had said.

CHAPTER XII.

IN HARBOUR.

THE weeks went safely by. The island of Madagascar was sighted and passed, and Mr. Hallers told Donny he guessed it would scare him to see the herds of cattle roaming through the rich pasture-lands. In the Indian Ocean, and along the Asiatic coast, hard winds from the northeast, called the dry monsoon, blew at times in a way to make the vessel struggle and strain with their fury.

At length, one fine morning early in April, they sailed into the harbour of Hong Kong, and Donny stood "amidships," so excited at the view before him he did not want to take time to eat his breakfast.

"Jolly! What a place!" he said to Mr. Hallers; "are there many harbours like this?"

"No, my son, not a great many. Why, bless you, my boy, this harbour is so immense, and has such safe anchorage, that the old salts declare all the navies in the world could be gathered here. What do you think of that?"

As soon as the anchor had been dropped, up and around the great vessel swarmed numerous small boats with Chinaman aboard anxious to make terms with the captain for taking him or any of the crew ashore, whenever they wished to land during the time they were in port.

A bargain was soon made with a boatman, and the captain explained to Donny that he must at once find the consignee, a man to whom a portion of the cargo had been sent. Then a stevedore would come, as usual, and attend to the unlading, and clerks from different trading-houses would soon be on hand, to see that things had arrived in good condition.

The captain had made so much of a companion of the "little mate" during the long voyage that he was somewhat surprised at finding how fond he had become of his company. He would willingly have taken the boy ashore at Hong Kong on the first trip, but he was not suitably clad to appear even in foreign streets. The second time he landed, the generous captain purchased such a supply of different garments, socks, shoes, and caps as, in Donny's eyes, appeared sufficient of an outfit for three boys.

The third time the captain entered the boat bound for the island of Hong Kong, the lad was with him;

and a little while before starting he had been made very, very happy by having his dear captain say to him:

"I notice, little man, you flounder about, now and then, scarcely knowing what to call me. 'Cap'n' comes rather hard to a boy of your size. Suppose you say 'Uncle Jack;' how would that do?"

"Splendid!" said Donny, the wideness of his happy little grin showing how great was the pleasure the question and the permission had given him.

Once landed, a pair of attentive young eyes took in the strange sights and sounds on every side. There were curious buildings, such as neither Donny nor any other little lad, coming from the other side of the ocean for the first time, had ever seen. They were open at the sides, with wide, flaring roofs like canopies: pictures of strange beauty they seemed, some two, others three stories in height. Uncle Jack said they were called "pagodas." Then he added:

"Some are places of worship, and some merely for show or ornament, as we say. They are gay, fanciful structures, such as the Chinese delight in seeing and visiting. Some of them are considered quite sacred or holy. We must go into one some day."

Most of the men were dressed in wide, flowing robes,

called tunics, loose trousers, and either wooden shoes or else shoes made of thick, soft felt. Many of the tunics were of figured silk, and some of cotton. When the weather was cooler the men had leggings drawn over the trousers. The pigtails were long and glossy, and, like Loo Sing's, were braided with great care.

Uncle Jack explained that Hong Kong was an island with several banking-houses and large trading-houses, which belonged to wealthy merchants, rich men, living in fine style at Canton, up the river of the same name.

"Some people call it the Pearl River," he said, "but it is more properly the Canton. My friend lives at Canton, and in a few days, as soon as the unlading is well under way, I shall go to his house. He would come to me at once were he sure of finding me. But I shall soon see my dear friend Richard now. I will take you along, my boy, and many a strange sight you will see in the rare old Chinese city. It once was the centre of trade for merchants and vessels, but since so many steamers run to Shanghai and Peking, the capital of China, way above here, the trade is much divided. But Canton still holds her own for importance;" and the captain laughed as though he knew all about Canton.

If Donny was extremely fond of following uncle

Jack about, certain it was the great, burly ship-master was very glad and willing to be followed.

"Seems like cap'n couldn't stir abroad, nowadays, without having that little poodle in tow," one of the sailors said to another, as Captain Jack and Donny were about to make the daily trip to Hong Kong.

"Don't know where he could look for a more lovin' little chap," was the reply; "pretty little marmoset, too, as you'll often find."

As a "marmoset" is a little monkey, it will be seen that Donny went for a very lively little fellow on the *Nanetta Masters*.

It was immense fun for the lad, going to and from the landing in the Chinese boat which the captain had hired for constant use. They slept on the vessel at night, but spent long, pleasant days at Hong Kong, the strange city of high mountains, with the town lying low down at their base. On rough, stormy days, when it was not thought best to go ashore, Donny could easily amuse himself "at home" on the ship, for to him it was a beautiful, great home. He would run down "'tween decks," where, like a mouse, he was once hidden away, and watch how fast the cargo was loosening and disappearing. Then he would run like a cat to the upper deck, and into the galley, where the sailors were eating from their tin plates, or pouring tea or coffee from the great tin pots.

He would scramble into the cook-room to talk with Loo Sing, whose "pidgin-English" flowed more easily since landing on his own shores. But it made Donny grow quite sober when, one day, the Chinaman said, with his wide, placid smile:

"Me no go sailee nex' time. Stay in Chinee. Get work in Hong Kong. Cookee for Melican man. Cappee get 'nother Chinamans do cookee on shippee. Me stay here."

Donny liked every man aboard ship, and every one was his friend. The gentle Chinaman had delighted in offering all kinds of good things to the merry little fellow, whose fair head and lithe figure were always welcome in pantry or cook-room, and the thought of seeing any one else in Loo's place was a real grief to Donny.

"Only think, Mr. Hallers," he said to the mate, that night, "Loo isn't going back with us. He wants to stay here, and says the captain must get another cook."

Mr. Hallers threw back his head and laughed. "Whisper, little mate," he said, in a soft, mysterious tone. "That China boy has sailed with Captain Spliffins going on six years. We've never made the

Chinese port once yet but he has decided to stay on shore. Just you wait till sailing time comes, and see the fun there'll be if captain takes it into his head to say, 'Loo, you can't cross with me, this voyage.' The poor fellow would go down on his little delicate hands and knees, and plead like an emperor to be allowed to go with us. He'd crawl aboard on all fours, sooner than be left behind."

Donny was chuckling with relief, and the drollery of the mate's words.

"But what makes him tell such a story, Mr. Hallers?"

"'Tisn't exactly a story, boy. The sight of his native land naturally makes him think he would like to stay home awhile. He tells, regularly, of staying ashore, whenever we land, and then, just *as* regularly, comes, a few days before sailing time, either to me or the captain, and says, 'Me sailee one more timee, one more timee.' I asked the captain, once, why he didn't make Loo think he had hired another cook in his place, seeing he had given notice that he wasn't going next voyage, but he asked, what was the use of breaking the poor fellow's heart for nothing? That's our Captain Jack, you know, out and out!"

Among other things, it amused Donny, every time

they landed, to have certain small traders come flocking up, thrusting trays or boxes before their faces, and urging them to buy " curus things."

"We won't trade with them, Donald boy," the captain said, "but when we go to Canton, I shall give you some money, and you can buy some pretty curious things for your own. You can fix them up in close brackets in the stateroom to suit yourself. I think it belongs to the right kind of a nature to like fine, tasteful things, and you must try and make the best choice you can. At Canton it will please you to go over my friend's house, and see the taste with which every room is furnished; for you will be allowed, I know, to roam about there as you please."

It had grown to be a great fascination — that means a great charm — to Donny, hearing uncle Jack talk of his dear "friend Richard;" he always spoke of him with affection, as if he loved him very much indeed, and whenever his name was mentioned the boy listened with heart and ears wide open.

"I want you to remember, my boy, as I have already told you, that this friend of mine — and I expected to see him before this, but have been detained — was determined to do well by himself from mere boyhood. He has two hands, two eyes, a good, cool head, and a strong, firm will. All these you have, my dear lad. It took a good deal of study, and as he had to work and earn money daytimes, he studied very often at night. Now he not only understands his own language better than a great many men do, but he has learned the Chinese and Burmese languages, which are very hard to master. I am sorry to tell you that poor Mr. Richard has had a very sad, lonely life of late years, but he is too much of a man to let sorrow make him forget or neglect the duty of each day. Learning is very much thought of by the Chinese, and they dislike foreigners very much, unless they are intelligent, — that is, good scholars, with bright minds.

"The mandarins, that is, Chinamen in high office, have but little to do with Americans or Europeans until they show themselves wide-awake, smart, able men. But friend Richard is connected with one of the great banking-houses at Hong Kong, and owns part of one of the silk factories at Canton, and is looked up to, not only by his own countrymen, but by men of rank among the Chinese."

Donny's eyes grew thoughtful, as they often did when uncle Jack talked soberly with him, and set him dreaming in a childish way, but the next minute the captain said, in his jolly tones:

"Haven't got to learn everything in a minute, little laddie, only catch hold of your reading and writing, and, by and by, arithmetic and geography. You ran to me for care and shelter, and I don't mean to shake you off. We must be looking out for a good school before long, — then we'll see how fast our boy can learn."

"Oh, and then I couldn't sail any more, could I?" cried Donny.

"Pooh! what of that, if you're getting ready to sail all right through life, my boy?"

The quiet smile that always sent an idea of the boy's fine little nature into the captain's mind, overspread Donny's face, as he said:

"'Twould be dretful hard to stop sailin' now, but p'r'aps I could stand it."

"There are people in the world who know much better how to teach little men their lessons than uncle Captain Jack," and the eyes twinkled merrily.

Again, as he had done once before, Donny went behind the captain, suddenly threw his arms about his neck, jammed his head against the broad back, and burst into sobs.

But this time strong hands drew him forward, and, placing him on his knees, with the fair head close to him, the captain said in firm, cheerful tones:

"Why, why! What's this? Cheer up, Donald, little mate; don't you know it must be months and months before all this precious schooling can begin? And you're not going to be a baby boy, and make it hard for uncle Jack, when he wants to make it easy for you, eh, little lad?"

Donny held his head up at once, but one lip would curl, all he could do. "You're so — so — good," he said, in little gasps, "and I — I loves you so!"

CHAPTER XIII.

AT CANTON.

At the end of another busy day, Captain Jack said to Donny, "To-morrow, my boy, we take the steamer for Canton; I've a breathing spell now, and before another night you and I will see friend Richard in his home."

As usual, when anything pleased him, Donny lay awake a little while, in his comfortable berth, thinking of the next day's trip, and how glad he should be to see "Mr. Richard." And when, in the mild, pleasant morning, he set sail on the steamer to ride up the Canton River, his bright eyes took in all they could see, at the same time he was asking himself some questions.

How would uncle Jack's friend look? Was he going to like him? And would his house be half as nice as the dear old vessel? But the strange vessels crowding close soon loosed his tongue, and set the questions running briskly.

"What are those, Uncle Jack, — those vessels like the ones we've seen, only so much gayer? My! ain't they fine though?"

"They're all Chinese junks, though of different styles," said the captain, as hundreds of the junks sailed along, their gilded masts glittering like sparks of gold in the sunlight. These were soon mixed with the pointed roofs of dwellings, and the delicate spires of tall pagodas.

At length they landed at Canton, and Donny had his first ride in a palanquin. The streets were so narrow, crooked, and full of children, dogs, men, and women, it would have been hard for a horse and wagon to get through them. Few are seen there. The captain stepped into the long, queer couch, — like a big rattan chair, Donny thought, as he scrambled in with him. There was a frame around the lower part, and a canopy overhead, and some silk curtains at the sides were looped up so they could look out. Four men, one at each corner, lifted the strange carriage to their shoulders, and ran along so swiftly Donny wondered how they ever managed to keep from trampling down the dirty little children that did not try to get out of the way.

He had plenty of time to see that the city was

divided into two distinct parts, one full of low, dingy, dirty-looking dwellings, some of them more like tents than houses; and everywhere were the poorly covered, miserable children playing in the mud, and taking no notice of anything that was passing by.

After going through several winding streets, they came to a part of the city where everything was changed. The houses were fine and large, although not very high. They had two or three stories, and were wide and spacious. Some were of wood, some of brick, and some of stone. Outside, they did not look as grand as the houses Donny had seen just once in New York, when a milkman gave him a ride "up-town." These finer houses were within walls, which now were old and broken, and appeared to be crumbling away.

They stopped before a large stone house, which Donny thought the best one he had seen yet. It looked like a fairy castle to the boy, who had never entered so fine a place, or, he thought, ever been so near such a place in his life. Before the house were flower-beds filled with pale, sweet lilies and rich, bright blooms. Shrubs, stunted trees, and plants with great broad leaves that Donny could have crawled under and been entirely hidden, were also growing here and there.

They went up a white shell walk to a wide piazza, covered overhead with a striped awning. There was no time to ask questions, for they were already standing before the open doorway, and a servant in a tunic of flowered, soft material was bowing low before Captain Spliffins, and holding out a lovely tray.

As the captain's card slid along the japanned salver or tray, the man bowed low again, smiled blandly, glanced with an extra smile, Donny thought, at him from his little slant eyes, and held out his arm at full length towards one of the rooms.

If Donny had gone into any well-furnished room, such as most people have in good homes, he would have seen things that to him would have been very beautiful. The cabin of the *Nanetta Masters* had thus far been the best place he had ever known, and it will be remembered he looked around in wonder at the captain's table, bookcase, and lounge.

But imagine a poor little boy going from Sunrise Court, with its broken chair or two, bare floors, and dull light on the dull walls, into the real sunrise brightness of a far Eastern mansion, and into the house of a merchant whose study it had been to bring together rare, beautiful things, and to scatter all over the airy, breezy house the rich and curious treasures of a wonderful kingdom.

When Donny seated himself on a low chair with carvings running all around it, Captain Spliffins thought the boy was so carried away with all he saw as to have forgotten all about the rest of the world. He sat near a window, where he could look across the garden, the shell walk, and the flowers; then he gazed, with a sleepy, far-off look, around the room, looked along the hall, gazed at the hangings, the entrance, and at the room itself. His face wore such a questioning, puzzled look, that Captain Jack said:

"Well, laddie, what do you think of it all?"

Donny turned quietly, smiled, and said, slowly, "Once, ever so long 'go, I guess, — I guess — *I dreamed 'bout this place!*"

They did not have long to wait by themselves. A quick footstep was sounding along the passage, and a gentleman with fair hair that was already slightly gray, a fine, soft complexion, and a tall, straight figure, appeared at the entrance, and came swiftly forward, both hands outstretched in welcome.

One said, "My dear captain," the other, "My dear Richard," then the two men shook hands as though they would never stop. After a few more words of greeting and welcome, Mr. Richard turned and saw Donny, sitting quiet as a little image, a smile just deepening the dimples in his cheeks.

"Ah! Who have we here?" asked the gentleman, surprised that he had not seen the boy as he came in, and fixing on him a look so keen that the blood came into Donny's little white face.

"That? That is the little mate of the *Nanetta Masters*," said the captain, his eyes all atwinkle, as he introduced his little lad. "His name happens to be Donald Hilborn, and I am his uncle Jack."

"Come here, my boy, and let me shake hands with you," said Mr. Richard, gravely; and as Donny went at once, and shook hands with him, the gentleman looked at the captain, and said:

"Let's see; somewhere about nine years or so, isn't he?"

"Yes, just about, I take it. You're about nine, aren't you, Donald?"

"Yes, I guess so," Donny replied. "Granny used to tell me I was eight; p'r'aps I've got up to nine now."

"Strange he should have that name," Mr. Richard remarked, as he looked sadly at the pretty boy, and drummed nervously on the table by which he sat.

"My dear little boy," he went on, "would you like

to see what I call my aviary, a room full of birds? They are quite a sight, I promise you. I'll have Wing Chin, my China boy who takes care of them, come and show you around."

Donny's face broke into a smile, and the gentleman paused in the act of rising, and, with his hands on his knees, looked sharply again at the boy's pretty face and sunny hair. "I like birds," he said; "uncle Jack had some on shipboard, and they know me, and I love them. I love everything on the ship."

"I guess you've got a warm little heart somewhere," said Mr. Richard, as he rang a bell. A well-dressed Chinaman appeared, and the gentleman said to him:

"Wing, please show this little gentleman the birds and the garden," and Donny followed the man, who led the way up a stairway with long, shallow stairs, which were very easy to mount. Every step or two he would look over his shoulder and smile. They went along a wide hallway with a shining floor, and rugs on which to tread. At the far end they came to a screen door, which the Chinaman opened, and Donny found himself in a regular bird chamber.

There were yellow birds, scarlet birds, black birds with crimson heads and breasts, and birds with feathers like Polly's, of green and gold. Some had long bills, some short; there were combs or tufts on the heads of some, others were sleek and smooth as a robin's. Some were singing, some chirping; others were plunging their plump little bodies into a tank of clear water, with white stones and green leaves at the bottom. Cages stood open, with cups full of seed in them, but the birds were flying all about the high, pleasant room. On an artificial tree in one corner was perched the most wonderful, exquisite creature Donny had ever seen. It stood on two slender little legs, its lovely feathers, of pale gold, hanging in a fall or cascade at each side, arched over, and hanging in long, bright, loose plumes. It was a bird of paradise.

For several minutes the boy gazed at it without stirring. Then he turned to the Chinaman. "Beautiful, isn't it?" he asked, with his quiet little grin.

"All velly nice," the man replied.

"Where did they come from?" asked Donny; "these fine ones, I mean."

The Chinaman worked his face with the peculiar expression, first smiling, then anxious, natural to the race when trying to find the proper words for a reply.

"They commce from allee over, allee over, velly far 'way," and he spread wide his arms, as if to point to the four corners of the earth.

"Yes, I know," said Donny, willing to help him out.

Meantime, in the room down-stairs, Mr. Richard was saying, " You know I never can see a little lad of that age without feeling all the old agony sweep over me, and that boy, with his soft little voice, and air of a little gentleman, reminds me so painfully of what that other lad might have been now! Where did you pick him up? And how came you to take a passenger aboard? I thought you were opposed to a charge of that kind. But I suppose some one coaxed you into it."

" No, he was a little waif that took passage of his own accord, just a wharf-bird that ran loose about the docks, where we were lying. I had shown a little common kindness to the boy," — Mr. Richard smiled knowingly, as if he knew all about the captain's big heart, — " and as I was to sail, just after his grandmother died, leaving him alone, and as some one had scared him nearly out of his little wits by telling him he had got to be a 'bound-boy,' he managed to smuggle himself in with the cargo, and three days out he came like a white shadow and threw himself on my mercy. We're a queer pair, but the little chap has got quite a grip on me, and makes a gleesome little companion."

" You'd better let me have him when you go

back," suggested Mr. Richard, with a slow smile. "I shouldn't object to seeing the little fellow around. There's plenty of room, you see."

"Couldn't do it, Richard. I'm too fond of having him about, myself. Plenty of room on the *Nanetta* for the slender chick, and I mean to educate the little man, and give him a good, fair start. But you shall have him here all you like while I am in port. I'll be generous to that degree, and be glad to lend my little mate where he'll be so happy."

"Oh, I don't know that it would be best," said Mr. Richard, sadly. "I don't want to get really fond of the little fellow, and I should be sure to."

CHAPTER XIV.

AN ORIENTAL HOME.

YET Mr. Richard did "get fond of the little fellow." For Donny was far too much interested in all he saw at the beautiful home not to be perfectly happy and contented to stay there as long as he could. When uncle Jack went to the vessel and Hong Kong for a few days, Donny knew he would soon be back, and when uncle Jack and Mr. Richard took trips together, they never thought of leaving the boy behind.

But it was into Mr. Richard's hand that Donny seemed now to most often slip his own, for the keen look that had first sent the blood to the boy's face had given place to so sad a gaze that the child felt it in his loving little heart.

Uncle Jack had told Donny, as they sat together on the piazza one day, that Mr. Richard once had a little son, who would be near his age if he had lived, but that both the boy and his mother were in heaven. "It makes him think of his little lad when he sees one of

AN ORIENTAL HOME.   161

the same age," uncle Jack had added, "but he enjoys having you near him."

Donny felt very sorry for Mr. Richard. He thought again of Timmy Sykes, of Red House Alley, who was a little, little boy, and he imagined how very bad poor Mr. Richard must have felt, to see his own little son lying all white and still as Timmy did, and the pity in the child's heart made him speak so gently, and creep so close whenever Mr. Richard came near, that the gentleman felt both the pity and the affection of the boy, and loved him for them more and more.

And so Donny was feeling as much at home in the fine house at Canton as he did in the cabin of the *Nanetta Masters*, and although Mr. Richard was not jolly like uncle Jack, but rather grave most of the time, he was just as kind as uncle Jack. And although his eyes didn't twinkle like a Santa Claus man's, his face would light up with a beautiful smile that made Donny happy every time he saw it, and he had a plain, easy way of explaining things that a boy could understand and enjoy.

Some things about the house of this rich gentleman, who had done so much for himself, became an everyday study to Donny. The great chairs on the piazza, or veranda, as they called it there, were of bamboo, a kind of light, hollow wood, like a reed, and were spacious, with high backs, broad arms, and long rockers. One was like a couch with a high top, making a place for a pillow, and had a lower part that could be pulled out so that a person could lie on it at full length, and was like a bed of willow ware.

All these chairs were delightful, even to a little lad who was almost swallowed up in any one of them. All around the railing of the veranda ran glossy vines, and Japanese curtains — really long lines of bamboo with beads here and there — hung at the sunny ends to keep out the heat while letting in the air.

In sitting-room and library were all kinds of foreign things, that Donny was free to examine to his heart's content. He was taught that the word Oriental meant Eastern, and that as China lay in the far eastern continent of Asia, it was easy to see why it was spoken of as being in the Orient.

Beautiful cabinets of japanned wood were filled with carved things in ivory and pearl, and many of these carvings were wonderfully fine, and must have taken a long time to finish. A complete little pagoda, also a perfect little vessel, were on one cabinet, carved in ivory. There were figures of men and women, of trees and flowers in these carvings. Then there were vases so fine and costly that Mr. Richard held them carefully while showing Donny that right on the fine chinaware were figures and flowers, held in place by wires so fine that the gilding covered them entirely.

Great China vases, with beautifully painted figures of men and women in Chinese dress, and nearly up to Donny's shoulders, stood either side of the broad mantels. There were black tables of lacquer (lacker) work, — that is, a thick varnish that grows hard, and shines like marble, — and in these were birds and flowers inlaid with mother-of-pearl, of changing colours, pink, and red, and gold, as the light shone on them.

Boxes of carved sandalwood, smelling sweet and strong, were all around, and great fans with splendidly carved sticks, silk embroidered, and with borders of white or coloured ostrich-feathers, stood against the walls, on the cabinet and mantels. Others, with delicate sticks and sides of carved pearl, had little porcelain faces on the silk part, and figures in Chinese costume of silk and satin.

There were no doors in the house except the outside ones, and the windows stood open most of the time. Fine silk hangings were at the entrances, but well looped away, as air is much needed a great part of the year. Chairs of sandalwood, with very high backs carved in all kinds of designs, were everywhere, and rugs were not wanting on the polished floors. Donny had to be careful how he went over the low, easy stairs, for he could see his face in them, they shone so, and he was likely to trip on the smooth surface, something the Chinese servants never did.

But Mr. Richard, who enjoyed giving the boy presents, handed him a pair of embroidered satin shoes, with soft soles, to wear in the house, and as soon as he went about in them he understood how it was that the Chinamen went about without the least noise, not a footfall being heard as they passed to and fro.

All the rooms, up-stairs and down, were large, spacious, and smelled of spicy woods.

The beds in the rooms up-stairs Donny at first thought were made of gold. They were of brass, and shone like gold. Here again were silken hangings, vases, chairs of bamboo, sandalwood boxes and fans, and bureaus and closets of camphor-wood.

One strange object in nearly every room was the "punkah," which Donny eyed in wonder. They were great fans of different sizes, used for cooling the rooms, and fanning people as they sat and talked, or as they ate. Some of them were hung from the ceiling, and were kept in motion by pulling a cord. Others were in frames which could be moved about the room. A servant was always in the room on warm days to keep the punkah swaying to and fro.

In the dining-room was the finest of linen, carvings, pictures; some of the pictures being painted on glass, in a manner peculiar to the Chinese, and others consisting partly of birds partially stuffed, and raised on the plain surface. The glass and silver were of the best, and the Chinese cook put such delicious things on the table that the dimples in Donny's cheeks were beginning to go further in whenever he smiled, his face was getting so round and plump.

At the back of the house was a garden with a high wall around it. Of this place Donny never grew weary. A couple of peacocks spread their magnificent tails with hundreds of "eyes" that seemed painted in shimmering green and gold. A flamingo, a tall bird with long, slender legs, and scarlet feathers tapering at the back to long, showy quills, strutted about, and it made Donny laugh to see it curve its long neck to look down at the proud peacocks. Two cranes and a stork or two, also long-legged, long-necked creatures, paraded grandly about, while several golden pheasants kept the peacocks company nearer the ground, their gleaming, yellow feathers in beautiful contrast with the flamingo's flaming plumage.

Wherever Donny went now, if Mr. Richard was not with him, a servant was sure to be close at hand, and the boy had only to turn his head if he wished to ask a question.

If he went either with uncle Jack or Mr. Richard for a walk or a little journey, as soon as they returned and were seated, — usually on the veranda, — a Chinaman would appear almost at once, tray in hand, with tiny cups of the finest chinaware filled with steaming tea, and with plates of crisp wafers, and some kinds of dried and sugared fruits. If a dainty table or stand was not already on the veranda, another servant followed with one in his hand.

It took poor Donny some time to get used to this. It was so strange that a little fellow who had no father or mother, no home of his own, or friends of his own, in the wide, wide world, should be staying on for weeks in a great stone house filled with all kinds of lovely things, with lots of servants to do the work, and look out for his comfort, and with no end of good things to eat; why, it *was* so strange he could scarcely believe in his good fortune.

"I'm only visitin'," he said to himself, "but rich

MR. RICHARD'S GARDEN.

boys would be glad to visit here, I'm sure they would."

One clear, warm evening, after Mr. Richard and Donny had been taking a walk, they sat outside, sipping sweet, hot tea, and Donny was nibbling at thin wafers and sugary fruit from the little inlaid table placed between them. In the bright moonlight Mr. Richard could see plainly the pretty, delicate face of the boy who sat enjoying his dainty sweets, and thinking how happy he was.

As the gentleman arose, and began pacing the veranda, he laid his hand on the child's head, and said:

"Well, little master, what might you be thinking of?"

The dimples went in, and the little grin spread over his face, as Donny said, softly:

"I was thinking God was taking elegant care of me."

Mr. Richard leaned over, kissed the lad's white forehead, and replied:

"I think you are a dear little boy, that's what I think!"

CHAPTER XV.

THE BOAT TOWN.

"Isn't this rather a warm day, Donald?" Mr. Richard asked, with a smile, as one morning Donny came down to breakfast with his little checked suit of light wool on.

"Yes, pretty warm," Donny replied, who had not felt uncomfortable, although the May sun was so warm that by noon the punkahs were swinging in lively fashion.

"After breakfast you had better go to your room, my boy, where Wing will have put some things on the bed that a friend of yours got yesterday, and I shall want to know what you think of his taste in dressing a small boy."

Donny's happy grin always said enough when he didn't know just what words to use; but Mr. Richard had gone away without him the day before, uncle Jack was off at Hong Kong, and all Donny said was, "A friend?" And the string of low giggles, with peeps at Mr. Richard's face, showed that he knew all about who the friend was.

"Oh, my! my!" he exclaimed, on going to his room, where the bed was really covered with the clothing and articles of dress spread on it. Wing Chin was smiling at the door, and all ready to reach for things when Donny wanted the use of long arms.

The first thing he took up was a suit of white flannel, so soft and fine he could scarcely believe Wing when he said it was "woolee, all woolee;" it was more like silk. Two nankeen suits, a material of loose cotton cloth, very prettily made, were the next things to be examined. "Velly coolee, velly coolee," Wing said of the nankeen, which was of pale yellow, and looked cool and comfortable.

A heavier suit of white flannel, with anchors worked in blue silk on the broad sailor's collar, was specially beautiful in Donny's eyes until he saw three blouses of grass-cloth, that were the nicest things in clothing he had ever handled. The grass-cloth was of the finest white material, so sheer one could easily see through it, and it had a crisp, cool feeling to the touch, really quite different from any other cloth. The collars and deep cuffs were exquisitely embroidered, not by machines, but by hand.

There was great beauty and luxury in these foreign fabrics or cloths; but the suits and blouses were not all there was lying on the bed. Three caps, one of white flannel, one of nankeen, and one of blue and white linen, matched the suits. There were also handkerchiefs, some of pina, and some of white China silk, like floss for softness.

Pina, which is generally pronounced "peena," is a material so very fine and thin, one can look through it like lace. It is made from the fibre of the leaves of the pineapple plant, and Donny thought the handkerchiefs were too "girly" for a boy to carry. But there was a long scarf of the same stuff to wind around the neck in cool evenings, which he liked very much.

On a table, in what Donny fondly called "my room," was a cover made of Shanghai gauze, so silky, light, and thin, the boy thought it a marvel how any one could have managed to work it, yet it was embroidered in all four corners with bright-coloured silks, and leaves and flowers were wrought on the cobwebby gauze that a puff of wind would have blown across the room.

Donny had fallen into the habit of calling his new friend "Mr. Richard," from hearing uncle Jack say "friend Richard," and as it rather amused both gentlemen, he was not taught to say anything else. Once in awhile uncle Jack would use some other name, which the boy did not take much notice of, and the servants had a jargon of their own, and seldom addressed their master in a way to call his name. The simple truth was, there were two very dear people in the world to Donny, at present, one known as uncle Jack, the other as Mr. Richard. Mr. Hallers was nice and kind, Sam Dickson, good and friendly. Loo Sing and Wing Chin were pleasant, smiling fellows the boy liked well. But no other men, anywhere, — and Donny was beginning to see a good many, — could compare, in his eyes, with his dear uncle Jack, and uncle Jack's friend, Mr. Richard.

Donny had been told that some time he should go with Mr. Richard to the silk factory, and also to "Boat Town," a strange kind of water city, some four miles away.

"You shall go into a joss-house, or god-house, for joss means god in Chinese," he also promised, "and into some of the pagodas."

It took more than one day, and required several trips to visit these places. In a beautiful joss-house, Donny saw something of Chinese worship, as the men fell flat before their carved idols or gods. Some of these houses are so sacred that no one but the priests are allowed to enter. But Donny went about with Mr. Richard, looking at the little ivory, wooden, and golden gods, and the fine things all around and about them.

A TEMPLE OR JOSS-HOUSE.

He laughed when Mr. Richard told of going by a joss-house, one day, and seeing a large god set outside, where every one passing by must see it. "I asked what god it was, and what it meant," he said, "and was told it was the 'rain god.' The rain was holding back longer than usual, and so the rain god was set out, either where he could see how much the rain was needed, or where more people would beg him to send the rain."

Even a child who knew as little as Donny did, felt the pity and foolishness of praying to such queer-shaped, homely gods as these.

At different times he went into several pagodas, where were also gods curiously carved, and almost no end of fanciful things placed about merely for show.

At the silk factory the boy was too young to have much explained to him. But it was a strange, interesting sight to see millions of silkworms wound up in cocoons, or outside coverings, which the worms spin from their own little bodies. Then there were looms that turned the thousands of thousands of yards of silk thread into the soft, pretty silk web that makes such tasteful dresses, and thousands of things besides.

Donny made more than one visit to the factory, and became so fond of going about, watching the process of reeling the silk from the cocoons, the poor worms having been first killed by heat, and of joining the ends in hot water, then of winding the silk on spools, or making it into the web or cloth, that he began to think there were other very pleasant ways of spending time besides being on or near the water.

But most strange of all was the day spent at Boat Town. The night before they were to go, Mr. Richard asked, "What would you think, my lad, of living on the water on a junk, or an old boat, or a raft, and never going on land from one year's end to another?"

"I guess I shouldn't like it much. Do many people do that?"

"Yes, thousands do, many thousands right here on the borders of Canton; they often live and die on the water, never touching land."

On the long, bright day when they set out for the visit to Boat Town, Mr. Richard hired a palanquin, and off they started at a brisk trot. As they were borne swiftly along, Donny found time to ask many questions.

"Oh, what has that man got?" and he pointed to a Chinaman jogging by, a bar across his back from which other bars hung from his shoulders, a bucket at each end.

"That? That is a milkman, and you would be surprised to see how full those buckets will be carried without a drop of milk being spilled. Now here we come to streets with queer names. This is Curiosity Street, because many curious things are sold here. Down there to the right is Glass Street, where glassware will be found in abundance. A little farther along is Bread Street, named for the bake-shops on each side, and still farther on is Fish Street, where all kinds of fish are sold.

"You see, we are getting into the old part of the city, where the people do not live very comfortably, because they are so poor. They have but very little money, and what they do have is not used very wisely."

"Do they drink rum?"

"No, as a rule Chinamen do not drink much liquor. But they smoke a kind of drug made from the poppy, called opium, which puts them into a dreamy state, in which they feel happy, and free from care or trouble. But the care and trouble come at waking-up time, when they are far too miserable and lazy to work, and have no wish for anything but to fill their pipes with more opium, and go dreaming off again."

Donny looked sober, then he grinned. "Polly would say, 'My, what a fool! What a fool!'"

Mr. Richard laughed, too. "Yes, and no wonder, Donald; I am glad to have Polly's pert speech come in where it works just right. There are a great, great many other Chinamen who do not use opium, — sometimes they chew it, — who are so ignorant, that is, they know so little, that they can only get the lowest, meanest kinds of work, and so they live scarcely better than animals. It won't be a pleasant sight that you will see to-day, my boy, although it may amuse you, but the time may come when you will be able to do something to help lift up the poor, and give them a better idea of living; then I hope you will want to. It is every man's duty who can."

They came to a place, after quite a journey, where Mr. Richard paid the men, and left the palanquin. They were near the river, where it was very muddy and dirty. Mr. Richard had on rubbers, and as he rolled up the lower part of his trousers, Donny saw he had on rubber boots. But what was the boy to do? The mud and mire were deep, and he had on only his neat, handsome shoes that uncle Jack had bought for him at Hong Kong.

But Mr. Richard knew what he was about. He said something to a Chinaman in the man's own language, and off he ran as fast as he could go. In a very short time Donny saw two other Chinamen coming with a sedan-chair hanging on a pole that went across their shoulders. As the chairs hold but one person, Donny saw it was for his use, and he was soon seated safely and comfortably; but they went very slowly, as at every step Mr. Richard had to pull his feet out of the mud. As the bearers of the chair were barefoot, they had less trouble.

Down, down they went, nearer and nearer the river, and soon they were in the midst of a great army of women, who were all digging in the mud. Slung on the backs of many of them were babies, peeping around with their little slits of eyes, and their heads bobbing about in such a funny way it made Donny laugh to see them.

"What are they digging for?" he asked, as the women, half-clothed, kept digging away, taking no notice of any one who might be watching them.

"They're after mollusks, Donald, a kind of shell-fish which they find in great quantities in the mud, which is their home. Many of them the women eat themselves; the rest they sell. They are a part of the population of Boat Town, and sleep almost anywhere, perhaps in a dugout, — a place dug out in the mud, with a few boards under foot and against the sides, — or they may have beds of rags on the hulk of some old vessel.

"All these people of Boat Town are called the 'Tankia,' and are really the water, or river, people of Canton and

China. But see the droves of children running about barelegged everywhere you may look; that shows that the air and the climate must be healthful, for there is but little sickness or disease among them."

They pushed on until they reached a kind of small pier, when Mr. Richard said something to the porters, but did not pay them.

"I want these men to be here with the chair when we come back," he said, "so I did not pay them. They would hang around all day and all night for less than I shall give them, so we shall be sure of finding your carriage on our return. Now, let's watch for a nice-looking boat; we can't sail very fast nor very far, but I want to get near some of the town boats."

"Here comes a fine one," said Donny, as a gaily painted, clean-looking little boat came gliding along.

Mr. Richard clapped his hands, the boatman heard, and at once swung around to the pier.

"Hop in, little man," said Mr. Richard; and in a moment they shot out into the water, but very soon were merely creeping along, winding in and out of the boats, junks, queer old vessels, hulks, and rafts, that, now they were fairly among them, seemed to have no end.

"Oh, what crowds and crowds and crowds of boats!" said Donny, as if the floating town began to look to him like the city it was. "Why, I can't see where they begin or end."

"How many boats do you suppose there are here in this river town, Donald?"

"I don't know. I should think a thousand."

"There are all of forty thousand boats, and more than half a million people. Some say there are not far from a million people, but I think that is putting the number too high. We're not in the poorest quarter, — I should not wish to take you there, — but we will see a little of how these poor Tankia live, and what they do for a living. I did not think to get you some rubber boots, so you will spoil your shoes, — but never mind, I'll get another pair, and, after all, the rubber boots would have tired your feet."

Mr. Richard spoke to the boatman, and they drew up to a raft and got out. On this, three men were fishing, and piling up the fish they caught in a rough box. Some women were working at a coarse net, sitting flat on the floor of the raft, and as many as half a dozen children were playing about. The men scowled when they stepped on board, but smiled at the piece of silver Mr. Richard handed them. Wherever they went Mr. Richard had the silver ready, and then they were free to go where they pleased.

From the raft a Chinaman helped them aboard a large junk, long, thick, and strong. Donny was surprised to see men, women, and children, ducks, chickens, geese, and boxes and boxes of eggs, crowding every part of this great vessel. The chickens were in rough coops, so were the ducks and geese; and such a cackling and squawking was going on that it was of no use trying to speak. The children were very dirty, the vessel was dirty, and there was nothing neat or clean to be seen. Rags piled here and there were, probably, the beds. No dishes were to be seen; Donny did not believe they had any.

From this they went to a strange craft, so queer in shape that Donny could not have named it, with all his knowledge of vessels and of ships. It had been a sailing vessel once, Mr. Richard thought, but the hold was the most there was left of it; yet an enormous place it was. Here puppies barked, and pigs squealed in such numbers that Donny laughed, and said, "This must be Pig Town, I guess." He had never seen so many pigs all put together in his life before, nor puppies either. The air was so foul here that both the gentleman and the boy were glad to get away.

Mr. Richard and Donny visited more than a dozen boats, some a little better than others, and on every one were men, women, and children, living in poverty, confusion, and dirt. They were, however, for the most part, busy. Many were fishing, a great many busy raising chickens, ducks, geese, puppies, and pigs. On some of the rafts one corner seemed to contain a kind of tent where the family could be sheltered a little at night; others had merely a pile of rags for beds, or a heap of straw.

"Oh, see," said Donny, as they both began to feel a little tired after their strange journeying from boat to boat, a piece of silver paying for the plank that took them from one to the other, "see, Mr. Richard, there is the clean little boat that brought us from the pier. How could the man manage to follow us about? Did you expect him?"

"Oh, yes, Donald, boy, the man would follow us to a much worse place than this, and one harder to reach, for the money I promised him to keep his eye on us, and we are only on the borders of Boat Town."

They sailed slowly back, and the first object Donny caught sight of, as they drew near the pier, was the sedan-chair, in which he was soon seated. Then they had to wait a few moments for a palanquin. The boatman bowed and smiled broadly at what he received in pay, and so did the bearers of the sedan-chair, who sent a palanquin that bore them close to home.

Ah, how beautiful the European quarter looked to Donny, as they reached the water side of it, with its walks neatly laid out, its trim shrubs, and fine trees! And how more than beautiful looked the stone house, with its covered veranda, wide chairs, vines, and urns, and the well-clothed servant going noiselessly and swiftly for the fragrant cup of tea!

CHAPTER XVI.

THE OLD POCKETBOOK.

"It's funny how poor some folks are, and how rich others get," Donny said, as he sipped his tea from the little gold-lined spoon.

"We only went to the edge of Boat Town to-day, as I told you," Mr. Richard replied, "but you saw enough to get some idea of the immense city of the Chinese who live all their lives on the water."

"So many chickens and ducks and puppies and pigs and eggs!" repeated the boy. "What can they do with them all? Do they sell them?"

"Yes, the Chinese as a nation are very fond of all kinds of poultry, fowls, pork, and eggs. Vast loads of all these are brought from Boat Town to feed the rich who are willing to buy, caring little for the dirt and filth midst which the things are raised. Ducks' eggs are a quite favourite dainty."

"Are the river folks good people?" asked Donny.

"Some may be good as they know how to be, my

boy; but many of them, both men and women, are very bad indeed. But the Tankia are not the only water-inhabitants we have in China. There are four hundred canals in the empire, and the Imperial Canal is a thousand miles long. These narrow streams filled with boats help out the narrow streets, and much of travel and trade is carried on by means of them. I think the people on the canals are, as a class, more decent and respectable than the Tankia. There are a great many classes of men and women in the great empire of China."

The next day uncle Jack was coming up to Canton, and, when he went back to Hong Kong and the vessel, Donny was going with him for a few days. Mr. Richard had told him that the next afternoon a "mandarin" and several gentlemen were to dine with him, and he would like to have him dress carefully in the best white flannel suit.

A mandarin is a Chinese official. They are rich, proud, learned, and keep much to themselves. They seldom dine outside of their own homes or the home of another mandarin, but Mr. Richard had lived in China fifteen years. In this time he had learned to talk with the Chinese in their own language, had become a very rich man, and had had frequent dealings with many of the Chinese grandees in the banking-houses at Hong Kong.

Donny saw by the preparations going on that the dinner was to be a grand affair. Wing Chin, the servant who waited most often upon him, drew up his face with an anxious look as he oiled the floors, shook out the silk hangings, and saw that another Chinaman rubbed the silver and polished the cut glass, wiped the pictures and mirrors, and sorted the fine table linen, until everything shone as brightly as it could.

"Great doings," Donny said, with his quiet grin, while watching Wing at his work.

The Chinaman's face was quite sober as he replied:

"Bigee bigee man commee! All velly bigee China-man commee get dinner. Fine dinner. All nicee, nicee, goodee, goodee, velly *first-rate!*"

Wing brought out the last two words in a tone of pride at having used English he felt sure of being just to the point, and quite up to date. Donny, always quick to laugh, gave a little burst of a chuckle at Wing's satisfied air, and the good-natured man smiled too, as if glad he had amused the boy.

The dinner, which was one of "state," was indeed a grand affair. Donny sat at the table without once speaking. Seven gentlemen were present. Most of the talk was in the Chinese language, but as two or three of the guests did not understand the strange, hard tongue, there was present an interpreter, a man who very quickly said in English what was said in the Chinese language.

Course followed course; first came soup, with parched squares of buttered bread, pickles, and crackers, then fish of so many kinds, and with such rich sauces, Donny did not taste of a quarter of them. Then poultry, game, birds, vegetables, and side dishes so many and so fine Donny began to understand why Mr. Richard had a great closet full of all kinds of beautiful plates, platters, and every kind of a dish that any one could ever want. Then there came puddings, pastry, cakes, and tea. After that, preserves, nuts, fruits of many kinds, and coffee. Lastly, ice-cream and little cakes made of all kinds of nuts, like our little macaroons, which are made only of almonds.

After that the table was cleared, and pipes of various kinds were brought. Some were called nargiles or hookahs, and had stems nearly a yard long, in which the tobacco is smoked through water. Tobacco in silver bowls was placed about, and a couple of crystal dishes with silver bands around them held a sweet, rose-scented snuff called maccaboy.

Donny was so tired of sitting, by this time, that he was glad to have Mr. Richard say, kindly, that the smoke might choke him, and he could be excused. He bowed like a little gentleman to each guest, as uncle Jack softly told him to do, then left the dining-room, and went up to the bird room, which by that time was lighted by candles, placed under glass covers and stood on high brackets fastened to the wall.

The bird of paradise was perched on the tree in the corner, preening his feathers that fell so gracefully at each side. Donny looked at it, and thought of the mandarin who had sat at the feast in a long, loose robe of brocaded silk, rich and costly, a thick silken cord, with heavy tassels, about his waist, a splendid diamond ring on his finger, and a kind of turban on his head, of embroidered satin, with a button in front, showing his rank as a Chinese gentleman and officer.

In some way the bird of paradise and the mandarin seemed alike to the simple mind of the boy. Both were showy, grand, and distant. "But I like the birdie best," said Donny; "his eyes are gentle; and with all his beauty, I do not believe he is proud."

The next morning, when it came time to start for the little steamer, Donny felt a pain at his heart at the thought of leaving Mr. Richard and his lovely home, even for a few days' stay on the vessel. He went, in his quiet way, to say good-bye, and wound his arms affectionately about his neck, which made Mr. Richard hold him close, kissing first one cheek, then the other, and telling him to be a good laddie, not to forget the house on land at Canton, and to come back soon. "See that you take good care of uncle Jack," he added, cheerily.

On the vessel there were jolly greetings as Donny ran to fo'c's'l, wheel-room, cook-room, and cabin. He pleased Loo Sing by eating a little dish of "lobscouse," a queer mixture of several kinds of meat and vegetables, all hashed together. But Loo had put in both curry and herbs, and a little dash of the fiery soy, — a dark, hot sauce made in China, — all of which made the minced mess, as Sam Dickson said, "mighty tasty."

Polly eyed him, with head aside, for a moment, then croaked, "Oh, how-dy-do, how-dy-do? Ha! ha! ha! Tie 'im up, tie 'im up!"

But little Jocko showed signs of real joy at seeing Donny back. He jumped to his shoulder, reached out a little paw and patted his cheek, then cuddled in his arms, blinking so contentedly and rubbing his little furry face against the boy's jacket, with what looked

THE MANDARIN.

like a kind of grin, that Donny took him on a short journey about the vessel, which the little animal appeared really to enjoy.

After supper, Donny and uncle Jack were sitting in the cabin, when the captain said, "Well, little mate, we've had a pretty good meal to-night, but not exactly the spread of last night."

This led to a talk, during which Donny said. "I keep a-thinkin' of the way the mandarin looked, and then of the Boat Town people. All is, if studyin' and learnin' all I can is goin' to make me a man like you and Mr. Richard, I'm goin' to study awful hard, and try to do as Mr. Richard did. He had money to give away, and he gave lots to those poor people where we went."

Uncle Jack nodded his head several times with twinkling eyes, which showed that he was pleased. "You're getting on the right track," he said.

The next moment, Donny and Jocko were having a grand frolic. The monkey rushed to the top of Polly's cage, out of the boy's reach, and this set Polly to screaming, angrily, "Clear out, you rascal! Clear out! Put 'im out! Put 'im out! Land! What a row! What a row!"

There was a great chattering, scrambling, laughing,

and leaping, when all at once Donny cried out, ruefully, "Oh, Jock, you naughty little fellow, you've torn my pocketbook!"

At that, Captain Jack, who had been half dozing, opened his eyes and looked around. "Oh, by the way," he said, "I must get you a nice little purse some day; then you might as well throw that poor old thing away."

Donny looked down, and began turning the worn pocketbook over and over, handling it very tenderly. "It was granny's," he said, softly, "and it's all I've got that was hers. If I ruther, I can keep it, mayn't I?"

"Why, certainly, my boy, of course you can. I'm glad to see you want to remember your grandma. You had better put that away carefully for a keepsake as soon as you have something else to keep money in. I wish you had something better to remember grandma by."

"I might tear up these old papers," said Donny, as he took a few old bits of folded paper from the pocketbook.

"See if you can read them, first," said the captain, who had tried, the last thing before Donny went to Canton, to teach him to read writing.

The boy unfolded several slips, which proved to be receipts for milk and baskets of coal. He made out very well in reading them, and as he was still spelling them out, a bit of old frayed ribbon, which was flatly folded, but looked as though it might have letters on it, fell to the floor.

In an instant, Jocko pranced over, picked it up, ran over to the captain, jumped to his knee, and handed it to him.

"Oh, you want to see if I can read writing, do you?" asked Captain Jack. "Very well, sir, we will try our best. Sit down, now, and give us a chance."

He put on his eye-glasses, unfolded the faded ribbon, and read. But after that there was no more joking with the cunning monkey.

Donny was not looking when the captain's eyes ran over the piece of soiled ribbon. He did not see the quick start, or swift, sharp glance, or know that uncle Jack was staring blankly at him as he went on studying the old bills.

Before the boy looked up, the captain was going over what he saw on the ribbon again, and it was several minutes before he moved or spoke. When he did, his voice was low and deep, and the lad before him was very attentive as he said:

"Donald, I want you to put on your thinking-cap, and see if you can remember anything about yourself when you were a very little boy. Think hard, now. Can you remember ever being in any other place besides Sunrise Court? And can't you think of some lady, perhaps, who used to hold you in her arms? Some one besides your granny, who might have been a great deal younger than she was?"

The boy's honest eyes turned towards the cages, the bookcase, the table, and back to uncle Jack. But nothing helped his memory.

"No, uncle Jack," he said, "no one ever took care of me but just granny."

"And don't you remember any woman at all, but her?"

"No one but old Mis' Mellin, that I stayed with after granny was gone."

"Can you remember her as long as you can your grandma?"

"Yes, I always knew Mis' Mellin, but she wasn't kind like granny was."

The captain sighed, slipped the piece of ribbon he had in his closed hand into his pocket, and told Donny it was getting late, and he had better go to his berth.

"I shall go back to Canton in the morning," he

said. "I have business that must be looked after right away."

"May I go with you, uncle Jack?"

The captain looked down a moment, and seemed to be thinking.

"Yes, Donald, I think you had better go with me."

CHAPTER XVII.

THE PIECE OF SATIN RIBBON.

"Now, this *is* a pleasure!" said Mr. Richard, his face lighting up as it only did at rare times.

He was sitting on the side of the veranda, reading and smoking, when his ear caught the sound of footsteps on the shell walk, and there was Captain Jack rolling towards the house, and Donny skipping along beside him.

He went quickly to meet them, tossed Donny to his shoulder, and shook hands with the captain as heartily as though he had not seen him for a month.

"Got homesick so soon, eh, old boy?" he asked, cheerily, as he pushed forward a chair for his friend, and put Donny down.

"Oh, yes, couldn't stand it but one night;" and the captain's eyes twinkled in the way it always did Donny good to see. "Had to come right back. Found there was some business I must talk over, the sooner the better; so here I am."

"He didn't get away without me," said Donny, with the quiet little grin that sent the dimples way in, and made his merry little eyes long and narrow.

"Good for *you*, little man," said Mr. Richard, stroking the fair head as if liking well the feeling of the soft, silky hair.

And there was Wing, smiling and bowing, a Japanese stand in one hand, and the usual shining black and gilt tray in the other.

"Seems beautiful, and all just like home," said Donny, who could not keep from smiling with happiness and content.

After finishing his tea and wafers, the little boy ran off to the garden, where he knew Wing would at once appear, and Captain Jack and Mr. Richard settled themselves with their pipes, puffing and chatting, until by degrees each grew silent.

The truth was the captain did not know how to begin what he had come to say, and Mr. Richard knew by his returning so soon there was some reason for it.

At length the captain said, slowly, and stopping to puff away the smoke between the sentences, "There was something happened last night, I thought I'd better come and talk over. 'Twasn't exactly a thing to write about."

"Always better to talk when one can," replied Mr. Richard.

"Yes, so 'tis. You see — that little mate o' mine was having a rush and tumble romp with our little Cape Colony monkey, when the little scamp tore an old, used-up pocketbook the child has always kept about him. I was advising him to throw it away, and promising a better one, when the lad said, with that bewitching little serious way of his own, that the pocketbook had been his granny's, and asked if he couldn't keep it.

"Of course I told the child to put it away as carefully as he chose; then, when he was about to tear up some greasy bills for milk and coal, I asked him to read them if he could. While he was spelling them out, Jock picked up a bit of satin ribbon, pressed so flat it looked more like tissue paper than anything else, but he brought it over to me, and — Dick, my boy, I've brought it here for you to see."

The captain's voice had grown a little husky, all he could do, and there was a sober twinkle in the kind eyes, as he handed over the piece of creased, frayed ribbon. He watched his friend out of the corner of an eye, as he unfolded the narrow strip and read.

The blood rushed up into Mr. Richard's face, and his strong white hand trembled, as he went over and over again the few words before him.

"Who was this old woman that the boy lived with?" he asked, after several minutes.

"Her name was Hilborn, and the boy thought his name was Donald Hilborn. After I saw that ribbon last night, I tried to find out if he could remember anything back in his little childhood, but he evidently could not. And when I asked if there was no other woman whom he could recall, he said no, no one but an old Mrs. Mellin I had heard him speak of before, a woman with whom he stayed, after old Mrs. Hilborn died, until he ran away to me. He remembers her as long as he does the woman he calls 'granny.'

"There is one other thing I want to mention just here," the captain went on. "When our little friend first sat in this room, I noticed he gave a slow look all around; turned his head so as to look at the walk outside, then scanned the room again, peered curiously into the hall and beyond it; then he said, in a simple, but puzzled way, 'Uncle Jack, once, ever so long ago, I guess *I dreamed 'bout this place.*' Now, we all know how anything will lurk in the memory, especially of a little child, and yet seem nothing more than a distant dream. He probably could recall no more, but we can put things together, and be pretty sure as to their meaning."

Mr. Richard's mind acted quickly. "Well, you know the story," he said. "Now, the only thing for me to do is to close the house, arrange about the servants, sail with you to New York, visit this miserable Sunrise Court, and find out what I can from Mrs. Mellin."

"We must take the boy with us," mused the captain. "He ought to be at school before long."

"I imagine he will never leave me from this on," and Mr. Richard's voice trembled as he spoke, "for beyond a doubt, my dear friend, it is my boy you have brought to me without knowing it; my own precious little son, come back to me the same as if from the dead."

"He brought himself, Richard. You must remember he ran from the court, where, I believe, with you, he never belonged, and made for the vessel that brought him here."

"Ah, yes! He came sailing over the seas to find his lonely, heart-broken father. He is my Helen's child, and, I tell you, Captain Spliffins, I am a new man from this day!"

"Queer how much at home the little fellow has felt

here," said Captain Jack. "I shall step back with all the grace my figger will allow. But I — I'd kind of made up my mind to have the loving little chap for my boy. Perhaps you remember I said as much."

"Well, bless you, you shall have a good share of him!" exclaimed Mr. Richard. "We won't say a word to him concerning our discoveries until we have seen Mrs. Mellin; although I know enough to satisfy me already."

"Come, little lad, bedtime!" called out Captain Jack, that night, in his jolliest tones. "I'm going over to Hong Kong early to-morrow morning, and shall leave you with friend Richard a week or two more; then — what do you think?"

"Are we goin' to sail?"

"Yes, boy, we're goin' to sail."

Donny's eyes grew big, and full of wistfulness, as he looked towards Mr. Richard. "I wish you was goin', too," he said.

"I am, my laddie!"

"O-oh! O-oh! Are you? Are we all goin' to sail together? Uncle Jack, and you, and me? Are we?"

"Yes, the whole crew of us," said the captain, who meant to kindly keep his own disappointment out of sight, and down deep in his heart.

"I don't see how I can spare you to go back to Hong Kong." grinned Donny, in a way to nearly close his eyes.

"Ah, you little villain;" and uncle Jack shook his fist at him. "You needn't be making believe you can't get along without me. You're in pretty good hands."

"Yes, but you were the first man to be good to me. I guess I sha'n't ever forget that!" And Donny looked very much in earnest.

"Well, well, be off with you to bed. This June sun is getting hot, hot! We must be on the voyage by the very first of next month, sure."

Two weeks glided swiftly by. Donny went every day, either with Mr. Richard or Wing Chin, for a walk, always amused by the sights on the way.

"Tellee fortune! Tellee fortune!" cried a strange object one morning, coming up to the well-dressed lad and his servant.

Donny shook his head for "no." He had been told not to have anything to do with the fortune-tellers, who, gaily dressed, and all smiles and bows, wanted to trace the lines in his hand, pretending to tell his fortune, for a little money. They met them often, and it was hard to shake them off, as they would follow,

"'YOU WERE THE FIRST MAN TO BE GOOD TO ME.'"

crying, " Me tellee goodee luckee! Me tellee goodee luckee!"

They also saw scores of porters, men with heavy loads on their backs, running in every direction. They were the expressmen of Canton, as of all Chinese cities.

Once in awhile Donny liked to go into a new joss-house where he had not been before, for there are more than a hundred in Canton.

" What lots of priests there are! " said the lad, during one of his walks with Mr. Richard, who always enjoyed going out with him when he could.

" Yes, there are all of two thousand priests and nuns in this one city," was the reply.

One day they went into a Mohammedan mosque, a great, gloomy temple Donny was glad to get out of. Another day they walked around the Confucian college, and saw a great number of Chinese students just filing around the walks.

At length the time came for the *Nanetta Masters* to set out on her return voyage. A man had been hired to look after Mr. Richard's house while he was away, and one of his servants was to take care of the birds and the garden. One night, Wing Chin came to Donny with a sad air, and with slant eyes downcast and mournful. Without the usual smile, he began:

"Pleasee ask cappee takee Wing on shippee. All velly muchee feelee baddee stay here; leetle boy, master, cappee. go sailee, leavee Wing allee lonee. Pleasee ask cappee takee Wing 'long. Me takee nicee care leetle boy: can cookee nicee in cookee-room. Pleasee ask cappee."

To this long speech for the Chinaman, Donny willingly replied that he would ask Captain Splitfins to take Wing on the voyage, and in his heart he hoped he would.

When he asked uncle Jack about it, his eyes twinkled. "Well, come," he said, "let's go see what Loo Sing says to staying over in China this voyage, and letting Wing Chin take his place. He has been saying he thought of taking a vacation."

Donny had returned to Hong Kong, and then had sailed over to the vessel that day, as they were all ready to start the next day but one. He did not look pleased at the thought of leaving Loo behind. He thought of the Chinaman's nice dishes, and generous ways.

"Oh, but I want Loo to go with us, too," he said.

"But I understand he has been wishing to stay in China, my little man. Never mind, let's go to the cook-room, and see what he has to say about it," and Donny followed the captain up the companionway.

In the cook-room, Captain Jack made Loo understand that he heard it was his wish to skip the voyage back to America, and that another Chinaman was waiting for his berth on the *Nanetta Masters*. "Had I not better hire him?" asked the captain.

Donny would have shaken all over with giggles of laughter, if it had not been for hurting Loo's feelings, at the dreadful faces the poor fellow made in replying. He must have forgotten everything he had ever said about remaining at home, for he spoke more quickly than was at all natural for him :

"Me feelee all velly sickee, stay so longee on land. Me stay homee some 'nother timee. Cappee no get cookee. Me makee all samee dishee for cappee. Me likee cookee. Shippee no go leavee Loo not yet."

"But it is such a good chance," urged the captain; "here is another man all ready to go. You've wanted to stop over so many times, why not try it now?"

The Chinaman put his hand over his heart, with a terribly wry face.

"Me die-e on a land. Sickee now, wantee water all saltee. Stay in Chinee long nuffee. Me go sailee some shippee if Cappee Spiffee no takee me 'long."

"Oh, well, that settles it, then. If you must go, you must, only I think it would be a fine chance to stay right here if you want to."

"Now you see, little mister man," the captain added, on the way back to the cabin, "we sha'n't hear a great deal about Loo's staying at home the next time we see China. A Chinaman has a good memory, and one good scare goes a great ways."

Two days later, the gallant *Nanetta Masters* had left the great harbour of Hong Kong, and was afloat on the China seas. To Donny's delight, both Loo Sing and Wing Chin were on board, for Mr. Richard had meant all the time to take his special manservant with him.

Folded very carefully, in Mr. Richard's inside vest pocket, was a strip of faded satin ribbon, and the words on the little narrow hatband were,—

"Donald Van Vere, Canton, China."

CHAPTER XVIII.

THE LAST OF SUNRISE COURT.

THE ship had sailed, as the captain wanted it to, on the first of July. She carried happy passengers, and a contented crew. Loo Sing was doubly pleased at finding himself in his familiar galley, and having a fellow countryman for company. All jealousy was kept away by knowing that Wing Chin took passage as a gentleman's servant, and neither as cook nor steward.

Uncle Jack had surprised Donny by telling him that Mr. Richard would take Mr. Hallers's stateroom during the voyage. "So you will have a new roommate, my boy, as the alcove part will still be your berth."

"But where will Mr. Hallers go?" asked the boy.

"Into the small stateroom beyond. Never you fear but he will be all right."

The vessel was making fair progress, when they were overtaken, in the Indian Ocean, by a hot, stifling air or monsoon, that grew worse and worse, until not a breath of air was left, and they found themselves becalmed. The great ship was as motionless as though she never would stir again, not even panting, as the sailors soon were, for breath. It was strange and unnatural to come to such a stand-still.

Donny thought this far worse than the storms he remembered so well. For five long days they lay perfectly quiet, not a breath of wind stirring, while it was so hot it was all they could do just to live with what patience they could, and hope for a change.

The bo's'n put up a dog-vane, a little silk flag with a few feathers at the top of the stick, and Mr. Richard told Donny to watch sharp for the first faint stirring of the light feathers, or flutter of the flag. But day after day passed, the bit of silk drooped, limp and quiet, and not a light end of a feather moved.

It was nearly dark at nightfall of the fifth day that Donny, who was watching the dog-vane, saw a feather just stir, then another,—feebly, but still really stirring.

"Oh, uncle Jack," he cried, running to the quarter-deck, where the captain and Mr. Richard were lying, each with a pillow under his head, and trying to get up a feeble smoke at their pipes, "I've seen the feathers move!"

The captain started up, and calling Mr. Hallers, they went forward, and, sure enough, the feathers slowly lifted from time to time, and then the silk gave a faint flutter. This seemed to put new life into the whole crew, and a cry of thankfulness went up at the slight promise of the longed-for change. The wind rose gradually, until the bit of silk floated out straight, and a cheer arose from the sailors at the sight. Before morning the great vessel was again on her way.

Nothing of importance occurred during the rest of the voyage, except that Donny's lessons were taken up again, and were attended to by Mr. Richard, who was taking uncle Jack's place, more and more, with the lad, who did not understand why that should be. "I guess because Mr. Richard has the most time," he thought.

He was getting in the habit of asking Mr. Richard all kinds of questions, too, such as he had often asked Mr. Hallers or Sam Dickson. Little folks are very quick to find it out when any one likes to be questioned, and likes to teach them, and every day Donny learned something new from the gentleman he was learning to love better than he thought he ever should love any one but uncle Jack.

"Did you know, my boy," Mr. Richard said, one day, "that it was from the Greeks, the people of Greece, that the great mystery of the tides was first learned? They watched the water roll up to the shore in great waves, and then go back; and they studied it all out, then taught other people what they had learned. It was on the shores of this Indian Ocean they watched the tide rise and fall, twice in the course of an entire day."

When they were rounding the Cape of Good Hope, Mr. Richard said again:

"Perhaps you might like to know, laddie, that the Portuguese sailor, who discovered this cape, named it the 'Cape of Storms,' because of the rough tempests he met here. But a king of Portugal, called King John Second, changed the name to 'Cape of Good Hope.' Sounds better, doesn't it?"

"I should think the sailors would like it better," Donny replied.

It was just a hundred and forty days, from the time they left Hong Kong, that the *Nanetta Masters* again dropped anchor at Holland Wharf. It was a year since the homeless little lad had rushed up the gangway, and scrambled into a hiding-place on board the good ship, which had now brought him back again.

"I wonder what makes me feel so queer?" he asked, on going ashore with Sam Dickson. "Things look strange, — as if they'd changed since I saw them before."

"They always look that way after you haven't been seein' them for a long time," said Sam. "You've been lookin' at foreign shores, and foreign people, and your little eyes has got used to seein' everythin' different from what 'tis here. It'll take quite a spell for you to come round to where things'll seem natural-like, but pretty soon the old wharf, the streets, and all, will look just as they used to, and the strange feelin' will all go away."

A terrible wave of homesickness swept over the lad he did not like at all.

"Sam," he said, softly, and in a shaky voice, "Sam, I don't like it! I want to go back."

"Ho! ho! a great sailor you'd make!" laughed Sam. "Come, chirk up, boy! 'tisn't as if we was goin' to stay here for ever. Just wait till we get the silk and feathers, the tea, rice, preserves, the chinyware, and wot not, off this trusty old craft, and somethin' else on to her, then see how jauntily we'll hoist sails, and go ridin' over the water again!"

"You'll sail on the *Nanetta* next voyage, won't you, Sam?"

"Me? Catch me *not* sailin' on her! Why, child alive, Captain Spliffins is the finest man to sail with I ever knew of! He ain't a man to be trifled with,

— not a bit of it. But the *Nanetta Masters* is a good home for any man that's willin' to behave himself and be half a man; the captain'll help him the other half. As for you, little mister man, just look at the berth you've got! Mr. Hallers said the other night he didn't know which would get the biggest bite at you, the captain or his friend, but he was afraid that between the two they'd eat you up. So you'd better look out!"

Perhaps it wasn't very wise to tell Donny that, but Sam's jolly talk was just what was needed to make the boy feel better. Yet there was a down-hearted feeling he could not quite shake off.

Mr. Richard had gone ashore as soon as they landed, but said it was not best for Donny to go with him. All was bustle and hurry on shipboard, and the captain, who must attend to many things of importance, told Donny he could go to the wharf with Sam Dickson, if he chose.

"I'm goin' to see a crony or two," said Sam; "will you come along, or would you rather go aboard again?"

"I guess I'll go with you," said Donny.

It all came rushing back, as he went over the ground, that a year ago this was the happiest place of his poor little life, and all at once, while trudging at Sam's side, a rush of thankful feeling came over him. He was no longer in rags, no longer afraid that some evil boy would come and tear what few clothes he had off from him, and, — no, he was no longer afraid of having his heart broken by seeing the *Nanetta Masters* go sailing away without him.

So it was a bright-faced lad that met a few honest fishermen who did not seem as free with the well-dressed boy as they had with the little ragged wharf-bird, although they were glad to see him, and sung out cheery words of welcome. And, after all, the first day in port was quite a pleasant one for Donny; but it was with great joyousness he went with Mr. Hallers to the cabin, as it grew dark early, just as he remembered it had those other days when he used to visit the vessel, and hated to leave it as the darkness settled down.

He had a romp with Jocko, talked to Polly, who had a fit of the sulks and would only say, "Who are you? Who are you? Clear out, you rascal! Clear out!" and also enjoyed watching Loo Sing, who was talking briskly with Wing, and pointing shoreward. "I guess he is going to take Wing to see some friends, and show him the sights," he thought.

At night Mr. Richard came back, but was very quiet.

He took the boy on his knee, but did not have much to say.

The next day Donny went ashore again. Uncle Jack was busy with the stevedore, and Mr. Richard had left the vessel, going away by himself the same as yesterday.

"I wonder how it would look if I were to go and peep at Sunrise Court," said Donny to himself. "I kinder hate to; p'r'aps I better not." But he kept wondering on, as to how the place would look to him. "Guess I will just walk by, and see if it's just the same. There can't anybody steal me away in the daytime, and if they did, I'd run off and get back to uncle Jack and Mr. Richard again."

He was setting out, when a big boy came shambling along, and for an instant Donny felt like running away. But how foolish! There was great, strong uncle Jack only a few steps away, and Mr. Hallers, and two or three sailors, going to and fro.

It was Tony Winkers coming up,— Tony, whose voice had last been heard when he was trying to tell of the other boy hidden " 'tween decks " of the vessel he was being ordered off from.

Donny stood his ground stoutly as Tony drew near, and said, pleasantly, "How do you do, Tony?"

"Oh, my eye!" exclaimed the big boy, rudely. "Ain't you got to be the bloomin' piece, though! P'r'aps if I hadn't been fired off the ship I might 'a' been a fine gentleman by this time, all fixed out in fine

"'HOW DO YOU DO, TONY?'" SAID DONNY.

feathers and shiny shoes. Great luck comes in with the tide, doesn't there?"

"I wish you might have some good luck, Tony."

"Oh, you do, do you? Go to work and help me git it, then; you could, easy 'nuff."

"I wouldn't do anything wrong."

"Oh, I don't want any smugglin' o' me away on the raft, or anythin' o' that kind. 'Merica suits me well 'nuff fur a place to hang up my coat in. You could help me lots if you's a mind to. You must 'a' got in with a pack o' swells as has plenty o' money. I been tryin' ever'n' ever so long to git a kit for blackin' shoes. If you wish me good luck, gie me some money to help git a kit, and I'll — I'll thank you."

Here was a chance to help the boy, and show he had only kind feelings towards him, and Donny wished right away that he could do it.

"Well, I'll tell you what I'll do," he said. "I haven't got any money in my pocket, but, if I can, I'll give you some to-morrow. How much would it take?"

"I know a feller that'll sell me a chair, and a block, and his brushes, for three dollars. He's goin' into a store, and if I could git hold o' three dollars I'd be all set up, and be amazin' glad. 'Twould gie me a right fine boost."

Come to look at Tony when he was not cross, or doing some hateful, naughty trick, he did not have a bad face. Perhaps people had not been very kind to him, and now he looked so hopeful that Donny said:

"All right. You come here to-morrow, and p'r'aps I'll have the three dollars."

Tony actually smiled, asked a few civil questions, then ran away, whistling a gay little tune.

Sunrise Court came into Donny's mind again, and very slowly he started up the street, where many a time he had raced along with a fish or some fruit in his hands, and, on one joyful day, with the Santa Claus man's beautiful great oranges.

He went on, until right before him was the side street out of which was Sunrise Court. "Perhaps I'll see Tom Smart," he thought; but not a person he knew was in sight.

At length he peeped up the court. There were the broken planks, the rickety old steps, the shabby front door. He turned his head as a baker's wagon jingled by, and when he turned again — could he believe his eyes? — there was Mr. Richard coming out of the door!

The boy was so surprised that he never moved until the gentleman came up to where he was standing, and said, gravely, but with a glad ring in his voice:

"Come, my dear little boy, we will leave this place together, and we won't come back again."

CHAPTER XIX.

GOING HOME.

In the evening uncle Jack and Mr. Richard had a good deal to say to each other, and Donny had a feeling that for some reason they would like to be by themselves. But he must say something about Tony, and the promise he had made.

He was starting for the fo'c's'l, to find Sam Dickson, when he turned back, and asked, bravely:

"Uncle Jack, would you give me three dollars, please?"

"Three dollars, boy!" And the twinkling eyes opened very wide at the question. "Well, pray what does a little urchin like you want of three dollars? Did I ever!"

"I want to give it away."

"Give it away? And are you sure three dollars will be enough? Come now, are you?"

Donny laughed, and told all about seeing Tony, and what he had said. "I've got all nice and happy, and p'r'aps if Tony gets helped he'll be good and happy, too. I told him I'd give him the money if I could;" and the boy waited for an answer.

"Tony Winkers? Let's see; isn't that the chap that tried to take passage with me on the sly?" asked the captain.

"Yes, and he was a bad boy," Donny answered, honestly. "He tore my jacket, and snatched my fish, and used to say dreadful bad words; but he said p'r'aps if he'd gone on the vessel he'd been a fine gentl'man, too. He looked real pleasant when I said p'r'aps I'd get the money for the kit, and if I go 'way again I'd feel lots better to know I helped Tony, and he wasn't mad at me any more."

"I'll give you the three dollars, my boy," said Mr. Richard; "then if uncle Jack wants to help out with anything else we'll let him, won't we?"

Donny's eyes were just bright little gleams, as he said, "Thank you."

But surely there was something in the air that the boy did not understand at all. He had seen Mr. Richard talking with Sam Dickson a long time in the morning; and now Sam called him "Master Donald," and took on a respectful way of speaking that Donny only half liked.

After breakfast the next morning, Mr. Richard said

he would like to show him something in the state room, and they went in together.

"Did you ever see this before, my dear?" asked Mr. Richard, showing the piece of satin ribbon.

"N-o," said Donny, "I guess not."

"It was in granny's old purse. Look again; don't you remember it?"

"I've seen it folded up, p'r'aps, but I didn't know there was readin' on it."

"Well, take it now, lad, and see what it says."

Donny took the little slip and read, slowly, "Donald Van Vere, Canton, China."

"Now, listen, because I want to tell you a story in as few words as I can.

"Seven years ago I had a dear wife and a little boy living with me in the house at Canton that you know all about. I had been very sick indeed and was getting better, when my wife heard that her mother, who was in New York, was so ill that she could not get well. Like a good daughter, she wanted to see her mother once more, and, although I was not strong enough for a sea-voyage, I was getting along so well the doctor was sure I would soon be out again, but must be very careful.

"I was very sorry that Captain Spliffins, my friend,

with whom I had sailed more than once, was in mid-ocean when my wife had to start on her long journey; but she sailed with her little boy and a nurse in a fine, large sailing vessel, in the care of another good captain; as soon as I was able I was to follow her.

"By and by there came dreadful news. The vessel was lost, and only two men were saved, — two Portuguese sailors, who could not speak a word of English, and sailed right off again as soon as they could.

"Captain Spliffins was at Hong Kong with his vessel when the news reached me, and I was soon on my way to New York with him, where I was told again that only two men were saved from the wreck. I looked up what are called the records, that is, the report that is made about a wreck, but it was only the same story over and over again; no one came to land but two foreign sailors.

"But when I saw the name on the little hatband. it brought me to New York again, and I found from Mrs. Mellin that two strange sailors had stayed with Mrs. Hilborn one night, and made her understand they were from a wrecked vessel. One of them had with him a little child, that Mrs. Hilborn thought was his.

"In the morning the men had run away without

paying anything, leaving the little boy, in a flannel night-dress and a little cap, behind them.

"You see, they were ignorant men, who were, very likely, afraid to try to tell their story, for fear of getting into trouble, yet were too kind-hearted to leave the child to die when they could save it.

"When the 'Overseers of the Poor' heard of the little stranger that had been left at Sunrise Court, that Mrs. Hilborn said belonged to a sailor that had deserted it, — that means, ran away and left it, — they were willing to pay Mrs. Hilborn to take care of the child. She must have been able to read, because she told the boy his name, which was in the little cap. She did very wrong not to show the hatband to the 'Overseers,' but was, probably, very glad to get the money she had for keeping the child. And she may not have known enough to see that by showing the name some one might have learned of a little lost son. I am only very thankful she kept the satin band. Mrs. Mellin always thought the little boy belonged to the Portuguese sailor. And Mr. Dickson remembers about the wreck, and the story of the child, but he, too, thought the father ran away.

"Have you never heard people call me some other name than Mr. Richard?"

"I've heard folks say 'Mr. Van,' and sometimes a little more to it, but I thought it was the name they had in China."

Mr. Richard smiled. "You mean you thought it was the Chinese for it. No, laddie, my real name is Richard Van Vere. The name on the little hatband is Donald Van Vere. I had it printed myself, and I am quite sure you are the little son I lost seven years ago! You were nine years old the day we left Hong Kong. When you first went to the house in Canton, you thought you had dreamed of seeing it. *You had seen it!* The picture had been in your little baby mind, not in a way to exactly remember, but to make it dimly familiar, when you saw it again."

Donny's face broke into a sudden smile. "I did think I dreamed of it," he said.

"Now, you must not call me Mr. Richard any longer, you must learn to say 'papa,' because I am your father, and you are my own dear little son."

It certainly was a very lovely story, and it took Donny some time to realise that it was all true. But it is easy to get used to pleasant things, and the boy was soon dreaming, in the old way, of the delight it would be to go back to China as Mr. Richard's "truly boy." It helped make things seem more real as the story became known on shipboard, and Sam Dickson and the sailors touched their caps to him, and Mr. Hallers called him "little cap'n," instead of "little mate." But the heart of the child remained unchanged towards these jolly friends of other, poorer days.

Donny saw Tony Winkers only once after giving him the three dollars and some nice fruit uncle Jack had added. "I've bought the kit," Tony said, "and I'm doin' fine! I wish you good luck now, and sorry I plagued you so."

The words were awkwardly spoken, but did Donny's heart good. "That's somethin' else to feel happy 'bout," he whispered to himself.

One day he took his second ride "up-town," and his father showed him a fine house on one of the avenues. "That is where your dear, pretty mamma once lived," he said, "and as I had no relatives of my own, after my early boyhood, it was a great joy when I had a loving wife and a little son of my own. Do you wonder my heart broke when I heard that both were gone? I am very, very thankful that God has restored, given back my dear boy. I shall try my best to make a good man of my lad."

When Donny bade his papa good night, at the end of that day, he said, thoughtfully, "God did take care of me, didn't he? But — why didn't he take care of poor mamma, too?"

It was a hard question Donny asked, but his father answered, at once, "God did take care of her, my boy, even when he drew her to himself. He takes care of us all."

CHAPTER XX.

AT HOME.

On the voyage back to China, uncle Jack declared there were two monkeys in the cabin, instead of one. Yet Donny managed to settle down to three hours of study each day, as his father wished him to, and acted as teacher. But he still ran from galley to wheelhouse, scudding fore and aft, as sure-footed now as any of the sailors. Loo's dainties tasted just as good to Master Donald Van Vere as they had to Donny Hilborn. And although the boy had become "Master Donald" to the entire crew, he was the same merry little gentleman they had known on the previous trip out.

Into his active little mind, he was all the time storing fresh knowledge. There was just as much to be seen, and learned, the second time he crossed the Atlantic, as there had been the first. But the passage was a remarkably quiet one; both mate and sailors had many opportunities of explaining the working of the ship, and considerable about its machinery.

LITTLE MR. VAN VERE AT HOME AGAIN.

At Hong Kong, Donny could scarcely wait for the river boat that was to take them ashore. But here there was considerable delay, and Mr. Van Vere told the impatient boy it would do him no harm to learn to wait when he must. Wing Chin was sent ashore as soon as possible, with instructions to hurry to the steamer, and, once in Canton, to collect the other servants, that the house might be opened and aired, before the master and his little son arrived. Captain Jack would not be able to join them for several days.

They had reached port early in the morning, and, after what seemed a long, long time of waiting to Donny, they were rowed ashore. Not much time was lost in reaching the convenient little steamer, and all in good time he was back in beloved Canton. Some distance was travelled in a palanquin, then Donny begged to be allowed to walk. Yes, little master should have his way; the home-coming must be made as pleasant as possible.

He capered through the gate towers of the old city, made brave time in reaching the English quarter, and soon was in sight of the fine stone house. His feet fairly twinkled up the white shell walk, and his lordly little heels came down sharply on the broad veranda with a right gladsome ring.

He scarcely had time to notice how beautifully the flowers were looking in the great urns, how glossily the leaves of the vine shone about the railings, and how cool it was in the wide chairs under the awning, when there was Wing Chin, little japanned tables in hand, and, just back of him, another man, with tea, wafers, and sugared fruits. How could Wing have been so spry?

CHAPTER XXI.

LITTLE MR. VAN VERE OF CHINA.

THINGS had not looked so strange to Donny, on arriving again at the Chinese port and his beautiful home, as they had when he had landed at Holland Wharf. His father explained that this was because he had not been gone so long from China, for one thing, and then the newer scenes had made so deep an impression on his mind that they would not soon fade away.

On the return voyage, Donny had been much interested in a gentleman who had sailed as a passenger on the *Nanetta Masters*. He was still young, but had a careworn, unhappy expression, that made the cheerful child feel a great deal of pity for him. After a while he noticed that the man seemed to take great comfort in talking with his father, and with uncle Jack also, and before they reached the China seas, there was a change in his whole appearance. His face looked brighter, he moved about with a lighter step, and that beautiful bird of Hope must have found a place in his heart.

For a few days after his arrival, Donny was allowed perfect freedom to do as he pleased, then his papa told him that lessons must begin again.

"I suppose lessons are what make a man smart," the boy said, inquiringly; "but do they make folks happy, too?"

"I do not believe a person can be happy very long who neglects study, and I do not want my boy to make the mistake that some do."

All at once Donny asked, "Papa, what was it made Mr. Cushing look so sad, when we set out on the voyage? He looked happier before we landed."

"Perhaps that is the best question you could have asked me," his father replied, "and it may be that I could not do better than to answer plainly, and tell you a little about Mr. Cushing. When he was a boy of your age, he had a charming home, a rich father, and everything to make life bright and full of promise for the future. Did I say everything? No, he lacked one thing; that was proper ambition. That means a desire to get ahead, and make the most of one's best chances. This he would not do, would not study, would not do as his kind father wanted him to. He might have occupied almost any position in the business world that suited him best, had he only made application, that is, studied, and put himself down to his books.

"But no, what he wanted was a life all made up of fun and careless ease. As he grew older, all he cared for was going about from place to place, seeing the sights, and spending money freely for dress, and in the company of gay companions. A few years ago, his indulgent father died. Then it turned out that he hadn't as much money to leave as people had thought there would be, and his son found that if he was still to have good food and clothes he must do something to earn them.

"Well, my boy, he has had a hard time of it. He found it a relief to talk with your uncle Jack, and sometimes with me, and as we tried to encourage the poor fellow all we could, it probably made things appear more cheering than they had. He confessed he was all the time looking back, wishing that he could be a boy again, with the chance he once had, to study, to learn, to fit himself to take a *man's* place in the world. That was the secret of his sadness; it is what we call regret, or remorse, sorrow over something lost or wasted that cannot be had back again."

"Jolly!" exclaimed Donny, looking sober and determined, "I guess I wouldn't be such a big goose as that!"

"No, I should hope not, my boy, and you can see why I have told you this unhappy little story about Mr. Cushing. He has an uncle, who has been very ill, at Shanghai, and who urged his coming to China, to assist him in getting back to America. It may be that this uncle — who is an old acquaintance of uncle Jack's — may help his nephew, and I hope he will, for Mr. Cushing seems to have been more idle and thoughtless than really evil. We tried to show that life lies mainly before him, and a fresh start might yet bring success and happiness. But the fine chances of his youth are gone for ever, and he knows it.

"Now you've been hopping about from one country to another, seeing new, strange sights, all useful and instructive in a way, but I want you to be a little student, from this on. There will be plenty of time for fun, plenty of it, but I intend to keep on as your teacher for awhile; then, after getting you fairly started in what are called the rudiments, — that means the first simple lessons in different branches of learning, — I shall hire a tutor, a young man thoroughly able to instruct you in a regular course of study, leading up to where you can enter college, and, I hope, become fitted to be not only a prosperous, but a useful man.

"My boy!" his father went on, speaking brightly and sharply, "I heard a man say, once, that he had a friend who had a million dollars, which is a very handsome fortune; and yet he added that in another way the man wasn't worth a penny. What do you suppose he meant?"

Donny put on his thinking-cap. "I guess," he began, slowly, "the man didn't have anything else, but—just—money."

"Didn't have what, Donald?"

"Any kindness, papa, or any of the sort of stuff that makes any one want to help other folks. Oh, I know! He wasn't a bit like you, or uncle Jack."

Mr. Van Vere had to laugh. "You have the right idea, my boy," he said, "only you must never make the great mistake of thinking that uncle Jack or papa are above thousands of other men who try to do a little good in the world. You will find true men everywhere."

"Yes," replied Donny, "Sam Dickson was good and kind when he used to give the nice fishes that made a fine dinner for granny and me."

"Certainly he was, my dear, and I am glad to see

you remember it. Those who do what they can for others are always good and noble; but don't forget that the more a man has, the better he can do for others as well as for himself."

There followed happy days for Donny, mixed with study and hours for sport, just as his papa said there would be.

Then came a day when the boy's heart swelled with grief, and the tears would not stay back. Yes, it was hard, the first time he watched the *Nanetta Masters* sail off without him, with dear, dear uncle Jack on board waving a cheerful good-bye, Mr. Hallers and Sam Dickson shaking their caps high in air, and Loo Sing flaunting a red and orange scarf back of them all. A sudden recollection came back to Donny of the poor, pitiful day when he tried to return to Holland Wharf and let the great vessel sail away without him.

But the sad feeling lasted only a moment or two. For was it not his own wise, loving father holding his hand tightly within his own? And would not the safe old vessel come sailing up the China seas again, some welcome day, with uncle Jack and the other kind friends aboard, waving a joyous "Home again!" instead of good-bye?

"Ho! This isn't the least bit like that other day, when I thought everything there was bright in the world was goin' to leave me," Donny told himself, stoutly.

Then he began studying with a fresh will, and learned something new apart from his lessons every day.

On pleasant afternoons, the daintily dressed lad was often seen with his father on the famous Respondencia Walk, which in Canton separates the "Hongs," or English trading-houses, from the river. Here, on the broad promenade, they met people of many different nations and tongues, and the boy's many questions were replied to in a plain, interesting way by the intelligent man, who generally found it easy to explain whatever his little son might choose to inquire about.

The lad soon believed he could tell at a glance one of his own countrymen, however bronzed his face might be, or the sturdy Englishman, the brawny Scotchman, the jolly Irishman, the good-natured German, the polite, well-dressed Frenchman, and the dark, fine-featured Greek. He even learned, with an acuteness beyond his years, to distinguish a Shanghai merchant from a native of Peking. And he declared that in a short time he should know the people of Boat Town from the canal men.

"The poor Tankia are lower down," he said.

In the bird room Donny looks at the bird of paradise and says, soberly, "I have found out it is not *always* fine feathers that make fine birds. But that doesn't mean you." he hurries to add; for he loves the gentle bird, who knows him well, and is so tame he will eat from his hand. and is not a bit afraid when Donny strokes his feathers of gold or holds up the waterfall of graceful plumes.

In the garden the flamingo, with flaming quills. crimson and gorgeous as ever. still stalks proudly along the walks, looking down at the strutting peacocks. who flaunt their showy plumage as if feeling themselves for ever on dress parade. In the library. Wing Chin glides to and fro more noiselessly than ever. never disturbing little master when he is busy with his books.

A year slips by. The tutor has come. and is at his work. Something of the wisdom that is slowly creeping into our little boy's brain. shows in the delicate, refined face. People say he is growing to look much like his father. The father continually sees the mother's lineaments in the beloved little countenance; Donny himself thinks his face is like the beautiful picture that hangs in papa's room.

And now comes the day that Donny has dreamed and dreamed of for months, not in sleep, but in his own longing, affectionate little heart. He goes with his father aboard the Canton steamer with a radiant face, and feet that will not rest a moment. A great ship lies in the harbour at Hong Kong, three-masted, and flying the glorious Stars and Stripes. A river boat is coming up to the pier, and soon lands. Rolling from side to side comes one of the kindest, dearest of men, broad, tall, and noble. Two men shake hands as though they would never be done. Then the great-hearted ship-master bends towards the watchful, eager boy.

"And pray who is this little gentleman?" he asks, the old Santa Claus twinkle in his eye. And the lad nearly chokes as he answers, with a quiet, familiar little grin:

"If you please, uncle Jack, this is little Mr. Van Vere of China."

THE END.

www.ingramcontent.com/pod-product-compliance
Lightning Source LLC
Chambersburg PA
CBHW021819230426
43669CB00008B/801